THE COMFORT OF APPLES

THE COMFORT OF APPLES

MODERN RECIPES FOR AN OLD-FASHIONED FAVORITE

PHILIP & LAUREN RUBIN

LYONS PRESS
Guilford, Connecticut
An imprint of Globe Pequot Press

Lyons Press is an imprint of Globe Pequot Press.

Project editor: David Legere
Text design: Georgiana Goodwin
Layout artist: Nancy Freeborn

Library of Congress Cataloging-in-Publication Data is available on file.

ISBN 978-0-7627-5964-4

Printed in China

10 9 8 7 6 5 4 3 2 1

TABLE OF CONTENTS

INTRODUCTION

Most of our recipes call for a certain apple flavor i.e. "sweet," "sweet-tart," or "tart." Feel free to experiment within the chart. The chart is only meant as a loose guide. Also, a good "eating" apple is one that's excellent eaten fresh. Those are, by and large, good for salads. In baking, a dryer apple with low moisture content tends to hold its shape. A Granny Smith, for example, works well. "Subacid" apples have a lingering acidic tartness underlying the sugar.

The flavor context determines the suggested apple. A tart apple counteracts sugary desserts such as the French toast tarte tatin (page 124) and breakfast beignets (page 126), or sweet breakfast dishes like German apple pancakes (page 18) or apple pancakes (page 19). A sweet apple works well with salty dishes such as the lemongrass shrimp (page 56) or the Serrano ham tapa (page 35).

With wine, it's difficult to describe a bottle as simply "dry" or "sweet." Apple flavors are just as complex—each has its own degree of sweet and acid as well as texture and back notes. The chart is meant as a good starter guide.

Apple tasting chart

	Sweet-tart	Sweet	Tart	Eating	Pie
Akane	●			●	
Arkansas Black		●		●	
Ashmead's Kernel			●	●	
Baldwin		●			
Black Twig			●	●	
Braeburn		●			●
Bramley's Seedling			●		●
Cortland	●				●
Cox's Orange Pippin		●			●
Elstar		●		●	
Empire		●		●	
Esopus Spitzenberg	●				
Fortune	●				
Fuji		●		●	
Gala		●		●	
Ginger Gold	●			●	●
Golden Delicious		●			●
Granny Smith			●	●	●
Gravenstein	●				
Grimes Golden	●			●	
Honeycrisp		●		●	
Idared	●				●
Jonafree			●		
Jonagold	●			●	●
Jonathan	●			●	●
Macoun	●			●	
McIntosh		●			
Mutsu	●			●	
Newtown Pippin	●				●
Northern Spy	●			●	●
Paulared			●		
Red Delicious		●			
Rhode Island Greening					●
Rome		●			●
Sansa		●			
Senshu		●		●	
Spigold	●				
Stayman Winesap	●			●	
Suncrisp	●			●	
Tsugaru			●		
York		●			●

{THE ORCHARD}

"This plain act of snapping the fruit from the branch or lifting it from a wooden crate and drawing it up toward the ready mouth was an affirmation of the senses. To eat into the apple, to press the edge of the teeth past the taut unwilling skin into ready white meat, to feel the spray of tart and honeyed juices rain down against the tongue and wash over the palate was to know again how exquisite are the treasures of the ordinary earth."
—Frank Browning, *Apples*

It is a brisk, late fall day in the Finger Lakes region of New York State. Dennis Hartley sits on the porch fronting his orchard store, rising every so often to go behind the counter and ring up honey sticks, cider donuts, or bags of apples.

Resting his feet on a wicker trunk, he gazes over his orchard, which rolls away from the house down a gentle incline, offering views of the turning leaves that blanket the surrounding hills.

He is a man who loves to eat and cook, but he does so with a precision rooted in a sacred respect for ingredients. Perhaps this is the ethos of the farmer, who turns the soil, plants the seeds, tends the shoots, and trims the trees until that first fruit is born. Yet, like the vintner, the apple grower has a unique passion for flavor to go along with an almost electrically sensitive palate.

A discriminating palate is part of the orchardist's job description. There are over a thousand varieties of apples, and while the orchardist will never try that many, he makes his living tasting a vast range of the fruit. The apple challenges the taste buds; it makes you wonder what you're eating. Is it tart, sweet, sweet with notes of acid, or tart with lingering notes of sugar; juicy, dry, or somewhere in between? Is the skin smooth and delicate or rough and leathery; the flesh fine-grained or coarse; cracklingly crisp or tender and soft?

Examine the fruit before you take a bite: Is the skin as red as a stop sign or brown and scuffed as an old loafer? Is the flesh snow white and creamy, or bright pink, like the Pink Pearmain? The literary and botanical catalogue of apple flavor, texture, and appearance is seemingly infinite.

Combining botany, history, and the flavor classification of thousands of apples, S. A. Beach's *The Apples of New York* is considered a bible of the apple world. Many of the fruits are extinct, but Beach's clipped, exhaustive writing provides a window into the life of the apple fanatic. To crack open the pages of Beach's two dense volumes is to step into a world where the apple is king: a plush orchard where apples of all colors, shapes, and flavors hang from branches or blanket the ground. It is a place in which Beach and many others wander, notebook and paring knife in hand, measuring, dissecting, inhaling, tasting, and discovering.

Fastidious, even obsessive, Beach logs the origin of each apple, from sprawling orchard to humble backyard. These fruits have distinguishing marks, shapes, internal structures, and genealogies. The Isham apple "introduced in 1864 from the orchard of F.X. Phoenix in Delavan, Wisconsin is yellowish-green, mostly covered with brownish-red . . . the flesh is very yellow with veinings, firm, very sweet, and very good." Unfortunately, the Isham is extinct. (A side note about the Isham: Like many apples, the color on the shady side is different from that on the side facing the sun.)

Beach on the Blenheim apple: "the flesh tinged with yellow, rather firm, moderately juicy, crisp, moderately fine-grained or a little coarse . . . agreeably sprightly subacid, becoming rather mild subacid, good to very good, excellent either for dessert or culinary use."

Beach had (and still has) plenty of company. In seventeenth-century Britain, the peerage, with its vast acreage and staff, employed nurserymen who, working in greenhouses, raised hundreds of apple types and birthed horticultural societies, which often met to discuss their fruits. Connoisseurs, food writers, lavish eaters, the foodies of the time, they published books on apples, fruits, and desserts, written in the purplest of prose. Similar over-the-top descriptions can be found from the early to mid-twentieth century.

From 1929: "The Cox's Orange Pippin [a variety sold in many U.S. greenmarkets today] is a shade too sweet and rather floridly luscious and so lacks the austere aristocratic refinement that the Ribston exemplifies so transcendentally . . . beautifully soft but somehow insufficiently rounded and hence not quite perfectly balanced."

From a 1944 BBC broadcast: "There is in this noble fruit [the Blenheim Orange] a mellow austerity as of a great Port in its prime, a reminder of those placid Oxford meadows which gave it birth in the shadow of a great house in Blenheim. Like Oxford, it adopts a leisurely pace, refusing to be hurried to maturity or to relinquish its hold on life."

As times changed, apple growers and enthusiasts in Britain realized it was impractical to breed hundreds of potentially unpopular varieties. Instead, they gathered to codify the many types of apples, compare notes, and distill the most saleable and communally appealing. In the late nineteenth century, the Royal Horticultural Society Fruit and Vegetable Committee met and compared 1,545 varieties, identifying 60 that would, they felt, stand out as supremely marketable.

Simultaneously, American pomological societies were gathering both commercial growers and backyard orchardists to classify, taste, compare growing notes, and organize their collection of fruits. Sheer economy mandated they clean their desks and do some heavy editing. It was time to discern what would sell and what wouldn't.

And despite the dwindling options, the passion remains. Apple growers are a separate type, as dedicated to their product as the royal horticulturists of yore. Decades, even centuries later, Dennis Hartley sits on his porch, cool glass of home-pressed cider in hand,

and speaks wistfully of the bliss of a perfectly cooked salmon with an apple chutney. Or the "snappiness" of turned cider, which he creates by keeping it in the refrigerator, partially capped. He takes a shot each day, sipping what soon becomes as tingly as champagne. Or the many uses of reduced cider and, of course, the near divinity of a perfect apple pie: "When people ask me about pies, I try to stress to them don't just cut up your apples and throw them in there! What fun is that? I mean, you're making a pie; presentation is everything with pies. Most people don't consider that. To me I tell them: take your apples, layer them in there; add maybe a layer of pears, or different flavored apples; give it a complexity."

We'll revisit pies, but one only has to hear the grace in his voice to understand the place that apples hold in his heart. Again, it is a pride only the grower can know, for, put simply, it is not easy to grow an apple. In fact, it takes a skill developed over centuries, a rare merger of art and science.

If, one day, after munching a Fuji apple, you head for the backyard and plant its seeds (odds are you won't get apples), you will not end up with a tree full of Fuji apples. This simple quirk of nature, an odd little twist inside an odd little seed (charmingly referred to as a "pip" in pomological circles), has both frustrated and satisfied thousands of growers in thousands of orchards for centuries.

In order to guarantee your tree will provide a desired apple type, you have to employ the practice of grafting: The grower cuts a choice piece of wood from an existing tree (say, a Macoun) and grafts (or connects) it onto the rootstock of the same tree. The result is then planted, and in two or three years you have two Macoun trees, for instance. And so on. The trees in your local orchard have all been grown this way.

In his 1867 book *American Pomology,* Dr. John Warder illustrates how to graft an apple tree. He notes the most common methods: splice, whip, saddle, and side.

Splice grafting calls for the grower to carve a sloping curve in the desired wood and a matching reverse slice in the desired rootstock. The two are connected, puzzle-like, and then attached, using grafting wax and yarn, or other sealants. The other methods are similar in both function and purpose.

Weekend apple pickers may also notice that the trees are surprisingly short. These are known as "dwarf" trees, or trees that only grow to eight or nine feet. As Annie Proulx and Lew Nichols note in their book, *Making Cider,* the farmer can fit eight or nine dwarf trees in the same amount of space occupied by the old backyard apple tree. They lament, to a certain extent, over this inevitable product of modernization.

"The standard apple tree, tall, robust, and stately, symbol of a hundred memories in yellowed photographs of the old home place, is fading away. The big trees, like many things, have surrendered to the forces of progress. Gone is that first early-spring swing on the lowest branch, the fireworks of blossoms and sky-high robin's nest . . . gone, too, the aerial dueling with yellow jackets, the daring ladder-act routines; and gone is the up-the-ladder, down-the-ladder, boxing, sorting, boxing, and resorting for sale, for storage, for cooking, for cider."

Today's orchard looks different from what it did a century ago, though, as Proulx notes, "big is not necessarily best." The activity at Cornell's New York State Agricultural Experiment Station in Geneva, New York, is a case in point. Cornell's research center is the hub of our nation's apple study. Here, scientists oversee a catalogue of an orchard, raising hundreds of apple types, old and new. One can find a Zabergau Reinette (Germany, 1885), a Calville Blanc (the great French culinary apple first recorded in 1598), and many others, ancient and newborn, growing side by side.

Each apple seed contains within its hull its own unique net of genetic information; in this way the pip is a kind of botanical snowflake. The scientists in Geneva and elsewhere work to decode the DNA in apple seeds, pollinating, cross-pollinating, breeding, and crossbreeding in order to create the tastiest apple, which is also disease, weather, and insect resistant.

And they have invented many apples, some of which have for years remained nameless (such as the NY 429), some of which have become market standards. The Macoun, for instance, was concocted in 1923 by crossbreeding the McIntosh with the Jersey Black; the Jonamac arose in 1972 from a cross between a Jonathan and a McIntosh. Crossbreeding is not a wholly blind process. Specialists have managed to isolate the gene for, say, tartness. And when researchers grow a promising apple, as one farmer put it, "the folks up there [Geneva] go in a room and munch on apples all day till they get it right."

Many apples, such as the McIntosh (Canada, 1811), are "chance seedlings," or pure breeds so tasty and easily cultivated that they never required crossbreeding. Legend has it that years ago, "granny" was cooking with some apples and tossed the seeds out the kitchen window. Up sprouted a tree loaded with green apples, later named "Granny Smith."

Crossbreeding can be a remunerative activity. To the creator of the perfect apple go the spoils—or in this case royalties per rootstock sold. The Cornell folks birthed the NY 674, "a whale of a commercial apple," according to one grower, which was then sold to Mott's. Apple bandits have even been arrested trying to sneak into orchards in the dead of night on a devious mission to poach proprietary roots.

Our attempt to understand and manipulate this stubborn kernel is also part of its mystique. Even Shakespeare appreciated the blend of natural manipulation. Can we say the same of any other fruit?

You see, we marry
A gentleman scion to the wildest stock
And make conceive a bark of baser kind
By bud of nobler race! This is an art
Which does mend nature—change it rather; but
The art itself is nature

Nature has thrown another curveball in the way of the apple: a mind-numbingly expansive set of insects and fungi that bedevil the farmer. In his 1917 work, *The Manual of Fruit Diseases,* Lex Hesler indexed horrors and deformities complete with frightening black-and-white photos that belong in the pages of a medical school textbook: coal-black apples rotting from within, crawling with barnacle-like scabs and cratered from pitiless fungal foes.

To name a few: Bitter Rot is a fungus that washes down the sides of the fruit with the rain and enters any holes in the bark; Fire Blight attacks a fork in a branch and shoots along both paths, leaving behind a dead tree that appears charred, hence the name.

And then there are the strangely named pests: the Wooly Aphid, the European Leaf Roller, and the Speckled Green Fruitworm. Growers spray their orchards with pesticides; they also employ other weapons such as pheromone monitors, placed throughout the rows, which shoot pheromones to confuse the pests as they attempt to locate their mates. Of course, unanticipated cold or hot snaps are no fun. The same for hail, which, pellet-like, carom off the fruits, mercilessly denting and bruising the hanging apples.

To produce a single, juicy fruit, the apple tree and its tender must defy a multitude of foes, be they pests, fungi, weather, or, of course, the apple pip's matchlessly complex DNA. From Frank Browning's memoir of life on his family's Kentucky orchard: "An orchard in June is a banquet. It is a raucous feast laid out in a vast vegetative ghetto ruled by a continuous struggle over death and sex." However, successfully nurtured and picked, the apple-flesh, skin, even seeds can be transformed into any number of items, both sweet and savory.

{[COOKING WITH APPLES]}

"the spicy scent of banana, odor of cloves, full-flavored,
cream colored flesh . . . scented with grapefruit . . . clean,
pinelike, mildly tart . . . buttery, tastes of licorice"

—Roger Yepsen, *Apples*

Because of the modern Western world's surfeit of goods, we have no equivalent to the apple of yore: It's impossible to fathom a time in which our lives were so impacted by a single fruit. And yet, for the settlers in the New World, the apple was a crucial product. Apples were turned into applesauce, apple butter, and a variety of baked goods such as apple pie and apple pandowdy. There wasn't as much grafting going on: The settlers mainly used apples grown from un-manipulated pips, which produce apples that ripen earlier and don't keep as well, hence the need to pickle, preserve, and turn them into products such as apple cider and cider vinegar.

In his famous book *The Food of France,* Waverly Root reminisces on his journey eating and writing his way around that country, recording its regional products and dishes. Wandering around Normandy, Root found himself tasting a lot of apples and apple-based dishes. Indeed, for centuries, apples have been central to Norman culture: "Cider and calvados enter into many sauces which in other regions might be made of white wine, while the whole apple gets into other dishes. There is filet mignon . . . in which the steak Is accompanied with duck liver and cooked apples, doused with calvados and served flaming . . . a delicious, if rich, dessert is the soufflé, flavored with calvados, is stuffed with macaroons and a bit of cooked apple. Sugar is also made from Norman apples and used in candy . . . and to sweeten Champagne . . . and to make jellies, for apples are rich in pectin."

We urge you to look at an apple and think like a Norman. The apple is perhaps our most versatile ingredient, a culinary Swiss Army knife. It can be julienned raw in a salad; poached whole in spiced syrup; dried or fried as a garnish for cocktails and a canapé base; simmered into a compote; pureed as a side to potato pancakes; used in cider form as a deglazing or braising liquid; fermented into warm drinks; caramelized for desserts; and juiced then reduced into a glaze.

It can be cut any number of ways; it is used in virtually every ethnic cuisine; it spans the flavor spectrum from savory to sweet, playing a supporting or starring role in a dish. An apple tasting menu can open with a ceviche and finish with ice cream, the apple playing a starring and/or a supporting role in both. It spawns commercial products such as apple juice, cider, calvados, applesauce, apple butter, dried apples, and apple chips.

Of course, you also must savor the delicious classics. Dust a pie with cinnamon and cloves; sprinkle a cobbler with brown sugar; tuck wedges alongside a pork roast; puree it with pumpkin, butter, and thyme.

Try new apples, or even familiar apples grown in local, smaller orchards: The greenmarket Gala is entirely different from the supermarket version.

Find your nearest greenmarket or roadside stand, pick your own apples, or order them by mail. We think you will be surprised by their heightened succulence, crisp flesh, pleasantly challenging skin, and spicy aroma.

The best way to develop "apple taste buds" is to try different varieties. Host a tasting party: There surely will be disagreements, and this is due to the chemical structure of the fruit. An apple's flavor profile is defined by the ratio between sugar and acid. Professionals, from horticulturists to cider makers, use instruments to measure an apple's sugar and acid levels. But when it comes to tasting, each palate, be it amateur or professional, is different, and people prefer widely varying balances. While one taster may fall in love with the sweet-tart Greening, or the "pucker powered" Bramley's Seedling, another may recoil. All apples, no matter how sweet or tart, contain both sugars and acids. A sweet apple may not have more sugar than a tart apple, just less acid.

We disagree even about the texture we prefer in an apple. Dennis Hartley, the owner of Littletree Orchards, says: "People come to me all the time and ask for a crisp apple, and I'm stumped. What's a crisp apple?" Perhaps we just haven't been exposed to enough varieties to define "crisp." Our food vocabulary is much less clear than we think, but the more we travel beyond our tasting comfort zone, the sharper it becomes. As we try new fruits, vegetables, meats, fish, spices, and dairy, we know more of what's out there and what we like. For starters, take a trip to the greenmarket and scan the apples.

A greenmarket apple is sensually much more satisfying than your commercial apple. Hold it in your hand. Like a scuffed baseball, it has some texture, is slightly coarse, maybe even a bit pitted. Unlike a slick new baseball just out of the package, it feels interesting and beckons you to roll it around in your palm.

Like the Gravenstein, it may be yellow with a cascade of red and copper stripes. Or the Mutsu: green, oversize, and lopsided. We don't see the Arkansas Black anywhere but roadside stands and farmers' markets, but it is a beautiful dark red and considered one of the prettiest apples. True, it is a hard apple, but it has a pleasing and complex aromatic flavor. The Suncrisp is an excellent eating apple, though it contains perhaps a bit too much acid for the commercial market. Or the Golden Russet: smallish, brown, with a tough skin, on the dry side, and tart with an almost starchy flesh. On the other end of the spectrum lies the mild Keepsake, thin-skinned with a nice snap and mild sweetness.

Though you may not like many of these apples, keep tasting. You'll find exciting flavors, and come apple season, hunt down that fruit. There are thousands out there, many of which you'll never forget.

EQUIPMENT

For this book you need a well-stocked kitchen, i.e., sauté pans and saucepans of all sizes, blender, food processor, whisks, wooden spoons, and so on. You should also have a mandoline, melon baller, juicer, peeler, and food mill.

Mandoline: A mandoline is critical for a serious or even semi-serious cook. In our kitchen, we often reach for the mandoline before a knife. It is necessary for any recipe that calls for large quantities of thinly sliced produce (other than leafy items). We may be cooking several pies at once. Since our apple pies are sliced affairs, the mandoline saves time and gives us the uniformity we desire. We often use it when we need paper-thin slices for apple chips (page 30). There are two types of mandolines: Japanese and French. The Japanese is smaller and lighter. Both have interchangeable blades that allow you to cut uniform slices or finely julienne. Because the Japanese mandoline is so easy to handle and store, we use it all the time. The French mandoline is bulkier, but wider and thus better for larger items such as daikon radish. We use it when we need perfectly round apple slices, because a whole apple is often too wide for a Japanese mandoline, but for this book, feel free to trim your apple to fit the slicer.

Melon baller: Melon ballers are good to have for decorative purposes. To make a more interesting fruit salad, say, scoop balls from a cantaloupe and a few types of apples, and toss with a little lemon juice, sugar, and basil. A melon baller is particularly helpful with apples and other pitted or stone fruits: It allows you to scoop out the core neatly and quickly.

Juicer: We use bottled juices for most of our cooking. It's easier, especially when preparing large amounts of food, and they don't compromise flavor. However, as with our beet-cured gravlax, unless you can find beet juice in the store (and feel like spending a lot), buy a bunch of beets and juice them. If the juice is the star of the dish, as with our scallops and gelato, it's better to juice apples. Aside from the clean flavor of freshly juiced apples, you can control the amount of sugar as well as—with the help of some vitamin C powder—prevent the natural browning that occurs when you cut into an apple.

Peeler: If you'd like, peel the apples with a paring knife. But if you want to retain your sanity, use a peeler. Keep several in the drawer; in our kitchen they tend to break or get lost. Buy a Y-peeler, or one that looks like a Y with the blade spanning the tips of the Y. It's a much-improved version of your mom's straight peeler (my father, who consumes raw carrots by the bushel, refuses to switch over).

Food mill: Crucial for apple butter (page 136). While it's tempting to dump the pot of cooked apples into a blender, no amount of pureeing and straining will replicate the action of a food mill. The food mill is necessary for smooth mashed potatoes, but it is equally useful in picking clean the tough husks of certain fruits and vegetables, leaving behind a smooth puree. It should be used to make asparagus soup, for example. Machine-blended applesauce will invariably contain an unpleasant slurry of tough skin and seed bits.

CANNING

No book on apples would be complete without instructions on how to sterilize jars. You may want to store apple butter (page 136) or the autumn fruit jam (page 149), for instance. One method is to plunge the lids and jars in boiling water for fifteen minutes. Jam pros, like the folks at the Thornton Burgess Jam Kitchen, outline an exhaustive sterilization process involving scrub brushes, ammonia, and cheesecloth. While we defer to them in all things jam-related, thankfully they propose the alternative of running the jars and lids in the dishwasher on full wash cycle and full dry cycle.

CUTTING AN APPLE: A NOTE ON THE RECIPES

There are a few ways to cut an apple. For the sake of consistency, we use the same method throughout. An apple corer is a cute gadget, which we never use. Unless it is driven perfectly down the center, it always leaves remnants of tough core. Halving the fruit and removing the core with a melon baller is more accurate. If a recipe calls for an apple to be peeled and diced, do the following: peel the apple, stand it on end lengthwise, cut vertical slices to the required thickness. Do the same on the reverse side of the fruit and finish with the remaining sides. Discard the core. Turn into dice (or other desired cut).

If an apple is to be peeled, halved, and chopped, do the following: peel the apple, slice it in half lengthwise, use your melon baller to remove the core and any remaining stem, and chop. Use this method when cutting wedges.

And it's important to remember that most apples, especially small-orchard or greenmarket varieties, are not the same size. For this reason, most of our recipes call for cups rather than whole apples.

BREAKFAST

GERMAN APPLE PANCAKES 18

APPLE PANCAKES 19

POTATO AND APPLE LATKES 20

BAKED EGGS WITH CRISPY SAUSAGE 21

POACHED EGGS AND APPLE BUTTER 22

CRISPY DUCK AND EGG SCRAMBLE 24

People tend to be very particular about breakfast, especially when it comes to eggs, which we like cooked a certain way. Or our bacon, which we prefer at varying degrees of crispness; our toast; and, of course, our coffee. With pancakes, we simply want a warm stack of flapjacks coated with butter and syrup. These two recipes add warm apples to the equation. The German apple pancake is more crepe-like, while the other pancake is more traditional, though made even more melt-in-your-mouth by the heated apples. If you happen to be particular about breakfast, we offer you a pancake choice. For both recipes, a tart apple works best.

Ingredients:

6 large eggs

1½ cups sifted flour

¼ teaspoon salt

1 tablespoon sugar

2 cups milk

4 cups apples, peeled, cored, quartered,
     and cut in ¼-inch slices

Cinnamon sugar

Unsalted butter, for cooking

Procedure:

1. Beat the eggs in a medium-size bowl. Add the flour, salt, and sugar and whisk till smooth. Gradually whisk in the milk until combined. Transfer the mixture to a pitcher and let rest for 30 minutes.

2. Meanwhile, in a bowl, toss the apples with cinnamon sugar.

3. Melt 1 tablespoon butter in a large nonstick sauté pan over medium-high heat, tilting the skillet to coat the pan evenly with the melted butter. Continue to tilt the pan as you pour in just enough of the batter to coat the bottom. Working quickly, place several apple slices on top of the batter, then top with a little more batter to barely cover the apples. Once the sides begin to brown and bubbles appear on the surface, use a large spatula to flip the pancake and cook on the other side until lightly golden in color. Slide the pancake onto a large plate and cover loosely with foil to keep warm while you finish cooking the rest of the pancakes, adding butter to the pan as necessary.

4. Serve with jam, maple syrup, or more cinnamon sugar.

Yield: 5 large pancakes

Pancakes are often studded with a handful of blueberries or even chocolate chips. Blueberries have a limited season, and they can overwhelm, bleeding into and intruding on the pancake, transforming it into a blueberry disc interrupted by some batter. As for chips, melted chocolate is for dessert. Enough said. On the other hand, apples, when baked, turn subtler in flavor and play a warm, melting supporting part.

Ingredients:

1 stick unsalted butter, plus extra for cooking

½ vanilla bean, split, seeds scraped

4 eggs, separated

1¾ cups whole milk

2½ cups cake flour

½ cup sugar

2 teaspoons baking soda

Pinch salt

4 cups apples, peeled, quartered, and cut into ¼-inch slices

Procedure:

1. In a small saucepan, combine the butter and vanilla seeds. Place over low heat until butter has melted. Set butter mixture aside.

2. Meanwhile, in a standing mixer with the whisk attachment or a large bowl with a whisk, beat egg whites until stiff.

3. In a medium bowl, combine egg yolks and milk. Whisk in the melted butter, flour, sugar, baking soda, and salt, and whisk vigorously until mixture is smooth. Add the apples and mix to combine. Gently fold in the whipped egg whites.

4. Melt ½ tablespoon butter in a large pan over medium-high heat. Ladle in ¼ cup of the batter for each pancake. Cook until brown on one side and around edge; flip and cook until brown on the second side. Serve.

Yield: 16 pancakes

A NOTE ON FRESH APPLES:

For any preparation that requires a raw apple—such as a salad or a garnish—you need a certain type of apple. A great eating apple is just that—excellent when eaten from the palm of your hand: crisp, juicy, and any flavor you desire. A great eating apple is often ideal for raw apple dishes. However, we've all taken a bite of a snapping, crisp apple that explodes with juice, only to be let down by semi-soft flesh. It is best to use a firm-fleshed apple, even if it has a bit less juice and initial crackle.

POTATO AND APPLE LATKES

Phil used to work in a kitchen where he made a big batch of latke (no apples) batter in the morning, formed them into rounds, refrigerated them, and, in the evening, shallow-fried them for an hors d'oeuvre. However, we know them as a larger, crisp cake served as a side dish or snack. On its face, a latke is just a delicious fried potato. But if you think about it, latkes are more complex than, say, a French fry or *patatas bravas* (the classic Spanish tater-tot-like snack). They have an oniony bite and, in our recipe, an apple sweetness. They're best served alongside bowls of applesauce and sour cream, but they go well with a variety of robust sauces and condiments such as the chimichurri (page 75) or apple kimchee (page 143). The outside should be well-browned and quite crispy, but cook at a medium heat. Any higher and you won't cook the insides as well.

Ingredients:

1 cup peeled, grated russet potato

¾ cup peeled, grated apple

¼ cup grated onion (1 small onion)

1 egg, beaten

¼ cup plus 1 tablespoon flour

Pinch cinnamon

¼ tablespoon black pepper

½ cup canola oil

Salt

Procedure:

1. Preheat oven to 200°F. Line a baking sheet with paper towels and keep another tray near the stove.

2. Combine grated potato and apples in a large bowl. Squeeze as much moisture as possible from the onions, then add to the apple mixture. Toss to combine, then add egg, flour, cinnamon, and pepper. Stir until incorporated.

3. Heat 2 tablespoons of the oil in a large pan over medium heat. Using a ¼-cup measuring cup, scoop the potato-apple mixture into the pan, 3 to 4 per batch. Make sure not to crowd the pan.

4. Using a spatula, lightly press down on the latkes, spreading them into discs about 3 inches wide and ½ inch thick. Cook until crispy and well-browned on each side, 8 to 10 minutes total cooking time. Transfer to the prepared tray to drain and season immediately with salt. Place first batch on second tray and keep warm in oven. Continue with remaining batter. Serve hot.

Yield: 6 latkes

BAKED EGGS WITH CRISPY SAUSAGE

You could eliminate the sausage and make an equally tasty vegetarian dish. Baked eggs must be cooked in individual portions, which may explain their scarcity on the standard breakfast menu, but they deserve to be offered everywhere. Like an apple pie or a French onion soup, you break through the top to reveal a warm, savory interior. A sweet apple works well with the salty sausage.

Ingredients:

2 tablespoons unsalted butter

1 tablespoon sugar

1 cup apple, peeled and turned with
    a melon baller

1 tablespoon olive oil

1 cup hot pork sausages, casing removed
    (about 2 links)

¼ cup apple juice

6 tablespoons heavy cream

Pinch salt

2 tablespoons cream cheese

4 eggs

¼ cup grated Gruyere

Procedure:

1. Preheat oven to 325°F. Thoroughly coat four 4-ounce ramekins with 1 tablespoon of the butter and refrigerate.

2. Heat the remaining tablespoon butter in a medium-size sauté pan over medium heat, tilting to coat the bottom. Evenly sprinkle the sugar over the butter then add the apples. Shake the pan occasionally until the apples are lightly caramelized, about 8 minutes. Pour apples in a bowl and reserve.

3. In a small pan, heat the oil over medium-high heat until shimmering. Add the sausages, breaking them up with a wooden spoon as much as possible. Cook until dark brown and crispy, about 7 minutes. Add apple juice, and, using a wooden spoon, scrape the bottom of the pan to release the brown bits. Continue cooking until the juice has evaporated, about 1½ minutes. Remove from heat, add 2 tablespoons heavy cream and a pinch of salt, and stir to combine.

4. Remove the ramekins from the refrigerator and place onto a baking sheet. Spoon the sausage mixture into the bottom of each ramekin. Layer the apples and the cream cheese and crack one egg into each. Top each egg with 1 tablespoon of the remaining heavy cream and top with Gruyere. Bake until the yolk is cooked, 20 to 25 minutes. Serve.

Serves 4

POACHED EGGS AND APPLE BUTTER

Our apple butter recipe yields one quart for a reason: It's a great snack and also useful for this book. Apples have a lot of pectin, which allows them to thicken naturally when cooked down. The pectin really works its magic with apple butter, which is reduced for hours, resulting in a dense, jammy puree with no added sugar. It's a healthy alternative to béarnaise in an egg and bacon breakfast.

Ingredients:

8 strips bacon

1 teaspoon white vinegar

4 eggs

1 white pullman bread loaf cut in ½-inch slices, crusts removed, and toasted

1 recipe apple butter (page 136)

Salt and pepper

Paprika oil (page 35)

Procedure:

1. In a large sauté pan, fry bacon to desired crispness.

2. Meanwhile, fill a large pot with the vinegar and 5 quarts of water. Bring to a boil over high heat, and then turn down to a gentle simmer. Line a tray with paper towels.

3. Poach the eggs: Crack one egg at a time into a small bowl or ramekin. Slip it into the simmering water. Follow with the remaining eggs. Using a slotted spoon, gently nudge the whites toward each egg, keeping it together. Poach for 2 minutes and remove to the prepared tray to drain. (You can reserve eggs for later use by slipping them into an ice bath and quickly reheating later in simmering water.)

4. Spread each piece of toast generously with apple butter. Place one piece of toast on each plate, and top with 2 strips of bacon, followed by an egg. Season egg with salt and pepper, sprinkle a few drops of paprika oil over it, and serve.

Serves 4

CRISPY DUCK AND EGG SCRAMBLE

Duck and eggs. Delicious. When it comes to hash, duck confit is every bit the equal of corned beef or leftover Thanksgiving turkey. This dish works best when the duck is lightly browned but not dry. You don't need to reduce the cider to a thick, honey consistency. It should be a light syrup. Place a hearty pile of the duck meat atop the eggs, which should be creamy (see sidebar).

Ingredients:

2 legs duck confit

1 teaspoon cinnamon

Salt and pepper

2 cups cider

¼ cup olive oil

¼ cup chopped parsley

8 eggs

⅓ cup heavy cream or milk

3 tablespoons unsalted butter

Procedure:

1. Remove the skin from the duck confit but leave on any excess fat. Shred the meat into a bowl and mix with cinnamon, salt, and pepper to taste.

2. Bring the cider to a boil in a medium saucepan over high heat. Reduce until syrupy, about 12 minutes, and remove from heat. You should have ¼ cup. Reserve.

3. Heat the oil in a medium sauté pan over medium heat. When the oil is hot, add the shredded confit and cook, stirring, until soft and slightly browned, 8 to 10 minutes. Pour in the cider syrup, scraping the bits from the bottom of the pan. Mix well. Toss with the parsley, remove from heat, cover loosely with aluminum foil, and keep warm.

4. Whisk the eggs lightly with the cream or milk and 2 pinches of salt. Melt the butter in a large sauté pan over medium-low heat and swirl to coat the surface. Pour in the egg mixture and whisk continuously until the eggs are cooked to the desired consistency. Season with salt and pepper.

5. Divide the eggs among four plates, making a bed for the confit. Pile the confit on top of the eggs. Serve.

Serves 4

Scrambled Eggs

You're seated at a diner, sipping coffee from a white ceramic mug, letting your eyes wander from the glassed-in coconut cakes, lemon meringues, and giant fruit bowls with their attendant glacier of whipped cream. The short-order cook hovers over the griddle, frying bacon, sausages, French toast, and pancakes, and dipping speedily into a bottomless crate of eggs, cracking and scrambling, cracking and scrambling.

But what about those eggs? Too often, the diner scrambled egg is a plate of glum, dry nuggets. If you pay attention to the cook, you can see how that happens. He drops the eggs onto a volcanic griddle and proceeds to maul them with a spatula.

Scrambled eggs should be savory and creamy, cooked at a low heat and stirred constantly. Try these eggs and you'll stick to the pancakes and hash browns.

{ WHAT IS SOUR IN THE HOUSE . . . }

> "The Glass Apple is a species peculiar to Russia, where it grows in tolerable perfection. This apple is of a perfectly ripe form, and the skin, which is as transparent as green glass, shows the flesh through it. It is delicious to eat these ripe apples in the magical twilight of a Russian summer night."
>
> —W. C. Flagg, from the *Missouri Yearbook of Agriculture 1867 Annual Report*

Writers have, for centuries, rhapsodized over the apple tree. Dr. John Warder's *American Pomology* is a phonebook-thick dissection of the apple, from stem to seed. Yet, even in his microanalytic tome, Dr. Warder could not restrain his ardor: "The culture of fruits, and gardens also, contributes in no small degree to the improvement of a people by the excellent moral influence it exercises upon them . . . the rustic arbor, whose refreshing shade we have reclined to rest and meditate amid its sheltering canopy of verdure . . . the orchard, with its bounteous supplies of golden and ruddy apples, blushing peaches, and melting pears . . . such happy influences must have a good moral effect upon the young."

While one may debate the apple tree's power to straighten wayward youth, Henry David Thoreau had a similar, though more nuanced, take. In *Wild Apples,* he describes his experience with the unmodified apple: "It is necessary that you be breathing the sharp October or November air . . . in the fields when one is all aglow with exercise, when the frosty weather nips your fingers, the wind rattles the boughs or rustles the few remaining leaves, and the jay is heard screaming round. What is sour in the house, a bracing walk makes sweet."

For Thoreau, to confront a wild apple tree is to immerse oneself in a profound natural experience. Although viscerally affected by the moment, he declines—or is unable—to define the occurrence. All he knows is, one moment, strolling in the woods, he comes upon an apple tree, its fruit dangling in the clear, cold air, and the next, he is at his writing desk, munching a fruit whose flavor has mysteriously been transformed since being plucked from the branch, pocketed, and carried in out of the cold. Can it be? We inadvertently tested his observation.

One Saturday afternoon in late October, we drove our two-year-old son, Henry, to an orchard in the Hudson Valley, a few hours from the city. The air was clean and crisp, but the persistent light drizzle and sharp chill were enough to deter most visitors. Anyhow, it was very late in the growing season and most of the trees had been picked clean.

Nonetheless, we strolled through the vacant rows of Red Delicious, Macoun, McIntosh, and Mutsu, our eyes fixed high to the treetops, vainly searching for apples. We gathered a few from the ground, and we helped Henry bag and drag his bounty proudly along the damp soil. The apples, stragglers, having dropped of their late-season bloat from the bare branches, were very tasty. Back home, in a bowl on the counter, they went untouched and were soon discarded. The appeal was gone. Somewhere, Thoreau was smiling.

SNACKS, SANDWICHES, AND SALADS

APPLE CHIPS

Hors d'oeuvres should be satisfying to make and even more satisfying to eat. In creating our menus over the years, we've developed dozens of different hors d'oeuvres, separated into hot, cold, vegetarian, meat, and fish. Building hors d'oeuvres is a science: The items must be a certain size and varied in appearance and taste. One of the trickier problems is finding a vessel to hold this tiny bite. Apple chips are great for this purpose. When you remove them from the oven, they should be slightly pliable, but be aware that they become brittle quickly. Press them into small tart molds or use your fingers to create a cup, which can hold a fresh crab salad or spiced chickpeas. A Golden Delicious is mild and holds its shape in the oven.

Ingredients:

¼ cup sugar

1 cup water

1 Golden Delicious apple, unpeeled, sliced paper thin with a mandoline

Procedure:

1. Preheat oven to 180°F. Combine the sugar and water in a small saucepan over medium heat until the sugar dissolves. Pour into a large bowl and let cool.

2. Line two baking sheets with parchment paper. Dip the apple slices into the sugar syrup, coating well. Lay the slices on the baking sheets in a single layer.

3. Place the apples in the oven and bake until dry, about 2 to 2½ hours, checking occasionally. They are done when not completely firm, but still slightly flexible (they will crisp up in the air). To mold into a cup for an hors d'oeuvre, follow instructions in headnote. Gently lay them on a flat surface. They'll keep for several days in an airtight container.

Yield: 20 chips

CIDER-GLAZED NUTS

Toasted, flavored nuts invite one to experiment with flavors such as cinnamon and cloves, soy sauce, brown sugar, or butter, rosemary, and thyme. Done well, they're addictive. If you decide to use a blend of nuts, note that often they cook at different rates, so place on separate trays. They're done when they smell toasty. Try not to let them brown too much.

Ingredients:

2 cups pecan halves

2 cups walnuts

4 tablespoons canola oil

6 tablespoons apple cider

6 tablespoons sugar

2 tablespoons honey

Procedure:

1. Preheat oven to 350°F. Lay the nuts on a baking sheet and toast until fragrant, about 8 minutes. Remove to a bowl.

2. Line a baking sheet with foil and spread the canola oil evenly to coat the bottom.

3. In a small saucepan over medium-high heat, bring the cider, sugar, and honey to a boil and cook until the sugar dissolves and is syrupy, 3 minutes. Pour the cider mixture into the bowl with the nuts and toss well. Spread the nut mixture evenly on the prepared baking sheet, and bake until caramelized, 8 to 10 minutes. Let cool and serve.

Yield: 1 quart

PEANUT BUTTER TRUFFLES

A bowl of peanut butter and wedges of excellent, sweet-tart apples is a favorite snack in our house. Here, we've trussed it up. Make sure you refrigerate the mixture, as it softens in your hand. The finished truffles should be frozen to hold their shape. You can dust them before or after freezing. To dust frozen truffles, place them in a ziplock bag with sugar or cocoa and shake.

Ingredients:

1 cup heavy cream

1¼ cups crunchy peanut butter

1 cup unpeeled diced apple (⅛-inch dice)

1 cup pomegranate seeds

3 tablespoons honey

Confectioners' sugar (optional)

Cocoa powder (optional)

Procedure:

1. In a standing mixer with the whisk attachment, whip cream to soft peaks. Place the peanut butter in a large bowl and fold in the whipped cream until smooth. Fold in the apples, pomegranate seeds, and honey. Refrigerate until firm.

2. Line a baking sheet with parchment paper (you may need two baking sheets). Using a spoon, drop tablespoon-size dollops in rows onto the baking sheets. Freeze for at least 3 hours and serve, or place in an airtight container and freeze. They will last a few weeks. If desired, dust with confectioner's sugar or cocoa powder (see headnote).

Yield: 35 pieces

CROSTINI WITH CLAMS, BACON, AND APPLES

We spend part of each summer in Cape Cod, that rare vacation spot where the local food never gets tiresome. We're speaking, of course, of seafood: lobster, clams, swordfish, scallops, and so on. One night, we bought some fantastic littlenecks and came up with this crostini. The clam ragu is buttery and sweet and would be great on pasta or rice. A sweet apple complements the clams.

Ingredients:

2 pounds littleneck clams, well scrubbed of grit

½ cup water

1 baguette, sliced into ¼-inch rounds

⅓ cup olive oil

Salt and pepper

⅓ cup diced slab bacon (⅛-inch dice)

2 tablespoons diced shallots (⅛-inch dice)

½ cup peeled, diced apple (¼-inch dice)

1 tablespoon unsalted butter

3 tablespoons chopped parsley

½ tablespoon lemon juice

Procedure:

1. Preheat the oven to 350°F. Place the clams and water in a medium-size saucepan over high heat, cover, and let steam until the clams open, 5 to 7 minutes. Halfway through the cooking time, stir once from bottom to top so they cook evenly. When cool enough to handle, pick the clams into a bowl and strain the broth through a fine mesh strainer into another bowl, being careful to leave behind any grit. Set the broth aside.

2. Lay the crostini on a baking sheet in a single layer, drizzle with the oil, and season with salt and pepper. Bake until crisp and lightly brown, about 10 minutes.

3. Line a plate with a paper towel. Place a medium-size saucepan over medium heat, add the bacon, and sauté until crisp, 5 to 6 minutes. Remove with a slotted spoon to the prepared plate.

4. Add the shallots to the bacon fat and cook until lightly golden, about 3 minutes. Pour in ¼ cup of the reserved clam broth, and reduce until evaporated. Turn down the heat slightly, and return the bacon and clams to the shallots. Add the apples and ½ cup more of the reserved broth. Simmer until apples are tender, about 1 minute. Swirl in the butter and let simmer until the clams are heated through. Stir in the parsley and lemon juice and season with black pepper.

5. Spoon 1 teaspoon of the clams onto each crostini, arrange on a platter, and serve.

Yield: 4–6 servings

FRIED SHALLOT CROSTINI

An unlikely product of our Cape Cod summers: Once you start playing around with crostini, the options seem endless. Still, our crostini rule is to keep the flavors simple and avoid piling on a ton of stuff. This crostini requires a little attention. Don't burn the shallots. A good fried shallot should retain a sweetness that complements the apple butter (page 136).

Ingredients:

3 large or 4 medium shallots

2 tablespoons kosher salt

2 teaspoons chili powder

Canola oil for frying

1 cup flour

½ cup apple butter

1 baguette, sliced into ¼-inch rounds

1 tablespoon sesame seeds

Procedure:

1. Using a mandoline, slice the shallots very thin, separate into rings, and reserve in a bowl. Mix the salt and chili powder in a small bowl.

2. In a large pot, heat 3 inches of canola oil to 300°F. Line a baking sheet with paper towels. Place the flour into a bowl. In small handfuls, dredge the shallots in the flour, shaking off as much excess flour as possible. Carefully drop a small handful of shallots into the oil (don't crowd the pot or they will burn). After about 30 seconds, nudge them in the oil with a slotted spoon. They are done when light brown and crisp, 1 to 2 minutes. Remove to the prepared baking sheet, season well with the chili salt, and repeat until all the shallots have been fried.

3. To finish the crostini, spread a thin layer of apple butter on the bread, drizzle lightly with sesame seeds, and pile some fried shallots on top. Serve.

Yield: 24 crostini

Tapas are Spanish bar snacks, which have, over the last five or so years, become exceedingly popular on this side of the Atlantic. We like Tia Pol, a tapas restaurant in Chelsea. They're famous for a sea urchin roe and mustard oil sandwich, often called the best in New York. We love their dish of smoking hot charred green peppers, a tapas staple. Serrano ham is quite salty and lean. Fried, it becomes quite delicate and crunchier than the crispiest bacon, so try to find an equally crisp, sweet-tart apple. The ham is an alternative to bread as an hors d'oeuvre base. Straining the paprika oil makes for a beautiful red oil, but you don't have to strain, just try to leave behind the paprika at the bottom of the container.

Ingredients:

Canola oil for frying

½ pound Serrano ham, thinly sliced

½ cup sour cream

2 cups unpeeled, diced apple (½-inch dice)

1 recipe paprika oil (see sidebar)

Procedure:

1. In a large pot, heat 3 inches of canola oil to 300°F. Line a baking sheet with paper towels. Carefully add the ham a few slices at a time to the oil (it will shrink and curl). Remove after 20 to 30 seconds and drain on the prepared tray. Do this in batches; otherwise, the ham won't get crisp.

2. Place the ham chips on a platter, top each with ½ teaspoon of sour cream and 1 or 2 pieces of apple. Drizzle with a few drops of paprika oil. Repeat with remaining chips.

Yield: 24 pieces

Paprika Oil

2 tablespoons paprika

¼ cup olive oil

Heat the olive oil in a small sauté pan over medium heat. Add the paprika and immediately remove pan from the heat. Let cool a few minutes, then pour through a fine mesh strainer into a small container (see headnote). Oil can be refrigerated for up to two weeks.

Yield: ¼ cup

TANDOORI QUESADILLA

Quesadillas need not be Mexican. Our version is a bursting package of Indian spices balanced by a fragrant apple chutney. India has a robust apple industry, especially in Kashmir, whose elevation, rainfall, and temperate weather make for superb growing conditions. Orchardists raise Western apples such as Cox's Orange Pippin as well as local varieties like Ambri Kashmir.

Ingredients:

4 pounds chicken legs (6–7 legs), separated into thighs and drumsticks, skinned

4 cups apple juice

Juice of 2 lemons

5 cloves

1 teaspoon coriander seed

1 teaspoon cumin seed

2 cloves garlic, chopped

1 small onion, chopped

2-inch piece ginger, peeled and chopped

1 cup Greek yogurt

1 tablespoon tandoori food coloring (optional)

1 tablespoon salt

⅛ teaspoon fresh black pepper

8 ounces goat cheese, softened

½ cup minced cilantro

8 large flour tortillas

1 recipe apple chutney (page 138)

1 cup toasted coconut

Procedure:

1. In a large bowl, combine the chicken, apple juice, and lemon juice. Cover and refrigerate for 1 hour.

2. Toast the spices in a small saucepan over low heat until fragrant. Use a spice grinder or mortar and pestle to coarsely grind the spices.

3. In a food processor or blender, puree the spices, garlic, onion, ginger, yogurt, food coloring, ½ tablespoon of the salt, and the pepper until smooth.

4. Drain the juices from the chicken, and toss the chicken with the yogurt-spice mix to coat. Refrigerate at least 6 hours, or overnight.

5. Preheat oven to 400°F. Lift the chicken pieces out of the yogurt marinade, shaking off any excess. Place the chicken on a foil-lined tray, season with remaining salt, and bake for 25 to 30 minutes. When cool enough to handle, shred the meat into a bowl along with any juices from the tray. Fold in the goat cheese and cilantro.

6. Lower the oven temperature to 200°F. Place one tortilla in a large pan over medium heat. Scatter 1 cup chicken evenly over the tortilla, leaving a ½-inch border on all sides. Top with a layer of chutney, sprinkle generously with the coconut, and cover with another tortilla. Pressing lightly with a spatula, cook until browned on the bottom, then carefully flip and cook until browned on the other side. Turn onto a tray and keep warm in the oven. Repeat with the remaining tortillas. Cut each quesadilla into quarters and serve.

Yield: 4 quesadillas

BLT WITH CIDER AIOLI

Chefs, or even home cooks, like to tweak the classics: It was a happy day when someone thought of folding cheddar into biscuit batter. There are all kinds of substitutions and "deconstructions," some successful, some less so, such as one restaurant's short-lived fried Reuben sandwich. A BLT has seen many fine incarnations, but, except for the cider aioli, we pretty much stuck to the tried-and-true format.

Ingredients:

1 recipe cider aioli (page 144)

8 slices white bread, toasted

1 head romaine or Bibb lettuce, cleaned and separated

8 strips bacon, cooked to desired crispness

2 cups sliced apples (⅛-inch slices)

1 beefsteak tomato, cut in ¼-inch slices

Procedure:

1. Spread aioli over 4 slices of the toast. Layer the sandwiches beginning with one leaf lettuce, then 2 strips of bacon, a few apple slices, and one slice of tomato.

2. Top with remaining toast slices. Cut in half diagonally and serve.

Yield: 4 sandwiches

GRILLED CHEESE AND SPROUTS SANDWICH

Club Sandwich, in New Canaan, Connecticut, is Lauren's favorite sandwich shop. Specifically, the Number 41, a wrap of chicken salad, cream cheese, sprouts, and bacon. Freshly roasted chicken or turkey works best.

Ingredients:

8 slices white bread

4 tablespoons unsalted butter, melted

Apple butter (page 136)

Cream cheese, softened

Alfalfa sprouts

4 slices pan-roasted bacon

¼ pound thinly sliced fresh roast turkey

Procedure:

1. Lay the bread on a cutting board. Brush each slice with a thin layer of butter and flip it over so the butter side is down. Spread four of the slices with apple butter and the other four with cream cheese. Layer the sprouts, bacon, and turkey on the apple butter slices and top each with the remaining bread, butter-side up.

2. In a large sauté pan over medium heat, cook the sandwiches (they may need to be done in batches). When golden on the bottom, flip and cook until golden on the other side and the cheese has melted. Serve.

Yield: 4 sandwiches

OPEN-FACED THREE-CHEESE SANDWICH WITH APPLE AND PRUNE COMPOTE

Olivier Cheng, who catered our wedding, serves a luxurious grilled truffled cheese bite. We co-opted it for our menu, and since it's been such a big hit with our clients, we had to have a grilled cheese bite in the book. Put some thought into it: Sample a variety of cheeses, especially ones that melt well and have some bite. We like the following blend, which is sharp enough to stand up to the earthy sweetness of the cider and prunes, but you could experiment. Don't make a towering pile of cheese; the sandwich is best when thinly covered and sprinkled with the Asiago.

Ingredients:

1 cup prune-apple compote (see sidebar)

3 large ciabatta rolls, halved lengthwise

½ pound thinly sliced manchego

½ pound thinly sliced fontina

½ pound grated Asiago

Procedure:

1. Preheat the broiler. Spread a thin layer of the compote onto each slice of ciabatta bread, then top with a thin layer of manchego and fontina. Finish with a sprinkling of the grated Asiago.

2. Place the sandwiches on a baking sheet and place in the oven on a rack 6 inches from the heat. Cook until the cheese is bubbly and golden.

Yield: 4–6 sandwiches

Prune-Apple Compote

½ tablespoon unsalted butter

1 shallot, cut into ¼-inch dice

1 cup chopped prunes

2 sprigs thyme

1 teaspoon sugar

¾ cup red wine

¾ cup apple juice

1. In a small saucepan over low heat, melt butter. When the bubbles subside, add the shallots. Cook, stirring occasionally, until translucent, about 5 minutes. Add the prunes, thyme, and sugar; mix well. Pour in the wine and juice. Bring to a boil, turn the heat to low, and simmer until thickened and dark, about 1 hour.

2. Pour the compote into a blender or food processor and puree until smooth.

Yield: 2 cups

LENTIL AND CHARRED CORN SALAD

De Puy lentils come from France's Auvergne region. They're army green and the size of a very small pebble. Chefs like them for a number of reasons: They taste good, are quick-cooking, and hold their shape. You can serve this salad at any temperature; it feels a bit more substantial when warm, when the dressing soaks into the lentils. The best part of this salad may be the fried corn. The kernels become crispy and candy-like. Try to resist snacking on them before you've finished making the salad. A mild, sweet apple works well.

Ingredients:

1¼ cups lentils

1 carrot, halved

1 rib celery, halved

Half 1 onion

1 bay leaf

⅓ cup pecans

¼ cup olive oil

1 cup corn kernels fresh or frozen, thawed

1 cup baby arugula

1 recipe apple vinaigrette (page 146)

Salt and pepper

⅓ cup grated ricotta salata

Procedure:

1. Preheat oven to 350°F.

2. To cook the lentils: Add the first five ingredients to a medium-size pot, cover with several inches of cold water, and bring to a boil. Turn down the heat and simmer about 40 minutes. Stir from bottom to top and taste frequently so the lentils cook evenly and aren't overdone and mushy.

3. Spread the nuts in a medium sauté pan over medium heat or on a baking sheet to toast in the oven. Toast until fragrant but not too dark, about 7 minutes. (Be careful: nuts burn easily.) Remove to a cutting board and chop coarsely.

4. Heat the oil in a medium sauté pan over medium-high heat until shimmering, then add the corn. Let it sit for 1 minute, then stir or shake the pan occasionally until the corn is a deep golden color and crispy, 4 to 5 minutes. It may pop out of the pan so be careful. Remove corn with a slotted spoon and season.

5. When the lentils are done, drain well in a colander. Place them in a large bowl with the arugula, nuts, and vinaigrette and toss gently. Season with salt and pepper to taste. Sprinkle with the ricotta salata and corn. Serve warm.

Serves 4

TEA-STEAMED DUCK WITH COOL CUCUMBER

Our friend Hiroko Shimbo wrote *The Japanese Kitchen,* which belongs on every kitchen shelf. Her recipe for duck steamed in dashi and sake results in a duck breast tinged with the gentle smokiness of dashi. Using her dish as a starting point, we steam the duck in cider and tea, another take on this method. It, too, is a fragrant mix, which gently infuses the duck breast. Our duck is served both hot and cold: It is refrigerated, then partially seared to add some richness and texture to an otherwise cool, refreshing first course.

Ingredients:

1¼ cups apple juice

4 tea bags (Earl Grey or green tea)

2 duck breasts, about 14 ounces each, excess fat trimmed

1 English cucumber, peeled

2½ tablespoons fish sauce

1 tablespoon rice vinegar

1 tablespoon mirin

2 teaspoons sugar

1 tablespoon lime juice

½ clove garlic, peeled and minced

½ teaspoon red chili flakes

Salt and pepper

Procedure:

1. Preheat oven to 350°F.

2. Bring juice to a simmer in a small saucepan over medium-high heat. Add tea bags, remove from heat, and steep for at least 10 minutes. Remove tea bags. Let cool to room temperature.

3. Using a sharp knife, make a shallow crosshatch on the skin of each breast. Nestle the breasts skin side up, in a 9-inch round baking pan, or any pan that will hold them snugly. Pour over the juice, cover tightly with foil, and place in the oven. Bake for 30 to 35 minutes, remove, and let cool in the cooking liquid. Refrigerate.

4. While the duck is cooking, make the salad.

5. Slice the cucumber in half widthwise. Using a mandoline, thinly slice both halves down to the seeds, and discard the seeds. Stack the strips and julienne into ⅛-inch ribbons. You should have about 2 cups.

6. Make the dressing: In a small bowl whisk the remaining ingredients together. Add the cucumber, cover, and refrigerate for 1 hour.

7. Remove the duck from the cooking liquid, pat dry, and season both sides with salt and

pepper. Heat a medium sauté pan over medium heat, add duck skin side down, and sear until well colored and crisp, about 8 minutes. Remove from the pan and let rest for 5 minutes.

8. Slice the breasts thinly on the bias. Divide the cucumbers among four plates and arrange the duck slices decoratively within the salad. Serve.

Serves 4

We love a good bistro, from the menu written on the mirror to the red banquette and the zinc overtones. Bistros have been serving comfort food long before "comfort food" became ubiquitous. A winey coq au vin, rich moules mariniere, and a rare hangar steak with bordelaise sauce are all homey bistro mainstays. The flavors are deep and unfussy. We've updated the frisée salad, classically tossed with vinaigrette with or without bacon and blue cheese. The apple gelee is both surprising and refreshing. We use apple juice rather than cider, which is lighter in color and taste, more appropriate for a salad.

Ingredients:

3 (¾-inch-thick) slices crusty bread

½ cup olive oil

Salt and pepper

3 heads frisée, cleaned, trimmed, and separated

1 head radicchio

1 Granny Smith apple

¼ cup sherry vinaigrette (page 69)

8 tablespoons apple gelee (see sidebar)

Procedure:

1. Preheat the oven to 350°F.

2. Make the croutons: Tear bread into bite-size pieces and place on a sheet pan in a single layer. Drizzle with ¼ cup olive oil, season with salt and pepper, and bake until lightly browned, 8 to 10 minutes. Let cool.

3. Place the frisée in a large bowl. Tear radicchio into bite-size pieces and mix with the frisee. Halve, core, and slice the apple into ⅛-inch slices. Add to the lettuces and toss with vinaigrette. Season with salt and pepper.

4. To serve, place 2 tablespoons of the gelee in the center of each plate and smooth it out into a small circle with the back of a spoon. Top with the salad and croutons, arrange 4 or 5 apple slices around the plate, and serve.

Serves 4

Apple Gelee

1 cup apple juice
½ teaspoon powdered gelatin

1. Bring ¼ cup of the juice to a low simmer over a medium flame and remove from heat. Whisk in the gelatin until incorporated. Pour in remaining juice, whisk well, and pour into a small bowl.

2. Refrigerate until set, at least 2 hours.

Yield: 1 cup

CITRUS BEETS AND APPLES

We have a variety of beet salads on our menu. Although beets are a perfect winter root, they have a tender sweetness that transcends the seasons. This is a bright, simple salad, which balances soft beets with crunchy apple. A tart apple works well, adding even a bit more acid to the grapefruit dressing. Bottled juice is fine, but a fresh grapefruit is better as you should squeeze some pulp into the dressing.

Ingredients:

3 medium beets, about 1 pound, trimmed

¾ cup plus 2 tablespoons olive oil

Salt and pepper

2 tablespoons pine nuts

¼ teaspoon curry powder

Juice of one grapefruit, about ¾ cup

1 Granny Smith apple

2 cups sliced red onion (⅛-inch slice)

1 avocado

¼ pound bleu d'auvergne or other blue cheese, crumbled

Procedure:

1. Preheat oven to 450°F.

2. Place beets on a large piece of aluminum foil, drizzle with 2 tablespoons of olive oil, and season with salt and pepper. Wrap tightly in the foil and roast until tender when pierced with a knife, about 45 minutes. Remove and peel when cool. Dice in ½-inch cubes.

3. Line a plate with a paper towel. Heat ¼ cup of the olive oil in a small sauté pan over medium-low heat for 1 minute, then add the pine nuts and fry until golden, about 3 more minutes. Remove with a slotted spoon and drain on prepared plate. Dust with ¼ teaspoon salt and the curry powder. Reserve.

4. In a small bowl, whisk the remaining olive oil with the grapefruit juice. Season with salt and pepper.

5. Cut the apple into ¼-inch dice. Place the beets, apples, and onions in a large bowl and gently toss with the dressing. Cover and refrigerate for 1 hour. Divide the salad among the plates. Cut the avocado into thin slices and insert evenly throughout the salad. Sprinkle with cheese and curried pine nuts.

Serves 4

{ MODERN COOKING }

Apple recipes begin and end with a profound respect for the fruit. It is an iconic creature, redolent of the Garden of Eden and Isaac Newton. To this day, botanists regularly make a pilgrimage to the dense valley orchards of Almaty in Kazakhstan, the motherland of the apple, gathering the pips of these original fruits, destined for petri dishes and museum-like greenhouses. Their goal: to keep the past alive.

To respect anything is to study its history, and when creating apple dishes, one must acknowledge the culinary approach of those who, for eons, have been working with this product.

The Encyclopedia of Practical Horticulture is a compendium of fruit botany and crop management. Published in 1914, it also contains a collection of apple recipes. There are recipes for cakes, tarts, and lots of puddings. The dishes have interesting names, such as Apples en Surprises, and Jellied Apples with Almonds (a mold of jellied apples to which one affixes sliced almonds).

Tucked in among this collection is a recipe boldly titled "A New Apple Salad." The cook is instructed to poach a whole apple in sugar syrup, reserve and let cool; chop maraschino cherries and nuts and combine with whipped cream; serve the whole apple atop a lettuce leaf; and pour the cherry-nut mixture over the apple.

One can see how this creation was, in 1914, considered novel. At the very least, it is an apple salad rather than a dessert. No doubt it is a strange combination, but the strange often invokes the new. One can almost feel the author's mind straining for unusual uses for the good old apple. Unfortunately, she had a limited toolbox.

Like the 1914 author, we believe the apple deserves more than to be turned into pudding and pies, jellies and tarts. Unlike her, we have the advantage of time, globalization, and general culinary evolution. We have the freedom to pluck familiar and delicious recipes such as apple pie and German apple pancakes. But we also realize many cultures, hence apple risotto and apple kimchee. Apples and pork chops are a natural combination, but why not use other pork cuts, cider, and offbeat spices? Or fold apples into oatmeal for beignets, foregoing the traditional (yet worthy) batter-dipped fritter?

The apple works beautifully in so many dishes, one just has to bring it into the modern world, with an eye, of course, to the past.

APPETIZERS

BUTTERNUT SQUASH AND APPLE SOUP 50

OYSTERS WITH APPLE AND LIME GRANITE 52

HAMACHI CRUDO 53

SNAPPER NAPOLEON 54

LEMONGRASS SHRIMP WITH MINTED APPLES 56

"BORSCHT" GRAVLAX 57

ROASTED MARROW BONE WITH WARM APPLES 58

CHICKEN LIVER MOUSSE 59

PAN-SEARED *FOIE GRAS* WITH POMEGRANATE-APPLE VINAIGRETTE 60

BUTTERNUT SQUASH AND APPLE SOUP

Soup should be a smooth, friendly spoonful, which is why this is a lasting combination. Some ingredients just work well together: Butternut squash and apples have a complementary, mellow sweetness. Sweet potatoes and apples have a similar agreement, hence our sweet potato side dish (page 110).

Ingredients:

2 tablespoons olive oil

1 yellow onion, coarsely chopped

1 medium butternut squash, peeled, seeded, and cubed

4 cups apples, peeled, cored, and chopped

4 carrots, peeled and chopped

1 quart chicken stock (see sidebar)

¼ teaspoon cinnamon

Salt and pepper

½ cup walnut halves

4 ounces goat cheese, sliced in ¼-inch rounds

Procedure:

1. Heat the olive oil in a large pot over medium heat. Add the onion and cook until translucent, about 3 minutes. Add the squash, apples, carrots, stock, and cinnamon and bring to a boil, stirring occasionally. Reduce heat to low, cover the pot, and simmer until the vegetables are soft when pierced with a fork, 20 to 30 minutes.

2. Ladle the vegetables and half of the broth into a blender or food processor. Puree until very smooth. Return soup to the pot and stir in the remaining broth, one ladleful at a time, until you reach the desired consistency. Season well with salt and pepper.

3. To serve, place a few walnuts in the center of a soup bowl. Shingle 2 slices of goat cheese on top of the walnuts and ladle the soup around the goat cheese. The idea is to have the goat cheese visible atop the soup. (Hint: it may be easier to ladle the soup into a large measuring cup with a spout and pour from there.)

Serves 6

Chicken Stock

There's no substitute for homemade stock. Using it will make you a better cook, and one batch lasts for up to four months in the freezer. Order fresh bones from your butcher, but if they are not available, frozen will do. You will need a fine mesh strainer to ensure a clear stock; however, if you must use a colander, strain and ladle the clear stock from the top. Use a few pots if your largest is too small.

12 pounds chicken bones
1 celery rib, halved
2 large carrots, peeled and halved
1 teaspoon black peppercorns
2 bay leaves
1 medium onion, peeled and halved

1. Divide the chicken bones into two large pots, cover with several inches of cold water, and bring to a boil over medium-high heat. Boil for a few minutes and skim the scum off the top. Reduce heat to a low simmer and add the vegetables and spices, dividing them evenly between the two pots.

2. Let the stock simmer for 6 hours. Strain through a fine mesh strainer (chinois) into a large bowl and let cool. Refrigerate for 3 hours, then skim off any fat that has solidified at the top.

3. Pack the stock into plastic pint or quart containers. It will keep 4 months frozen, or 5 days refrigerated.

Yield: 5 quarts

OYSTERS WITH APPLE AND LIME GRANITE

Years ago, Phil and his friend spent an evening at Manhattan's Shaffer City Oyster Bar and Grill on 21st Street, downing tray upon tray of their marvelous oysters. Our favorites were the classic Wellfleet as well as the lesser known Hama Hama, Fanny Bay, and of course, the tiny Kumomoto. But go with whatever variety you like best. You can make granite with a number of juices. It's a kind of super-quick sorbet, which you can also spoon into a glass for a cocktail, although sorbet works better for that use.

Ingredients:

⅓ cup apple juice

Juice of 1 lime

1 teaspoon fennel seeds

12 oysters, shucked, on the half shell

Procedure:

1. Combine the apple and lime juices in a small bowl and place in the freezer. After about an hour, scrape the mixture with a fork to break up any icy bits. Continue to freeze, scraping occasionally, until it resembles icy slush.

2. Meanwhile, in a small sauté pan over low heat, toast the fennel seeds until fragrant, about 2 minutes, being careful not to burn them. Place the seeds on a cutting board and crush coarsely with the bottom of pan (let cool).

3. Arrange the oysters on a platter. Top each with 1 teaspoon of the granite and a light sprinkling of the crushed fennel seeds; serve.

Yield: 12 oysters

HAMACHI CRUDO

Crudo is an Italian dish of raw, thinly sliced fish—some types of shellfish can be used, especially scallops—dressed with some sort of acid, usually citrus juice. Some chefs treat it as a blank slate to which they add finely chopped quasi-garnishes such as pistachios and flavored oils. Whatever direction you take, the fish should be very fresh and very thinly sliced. Hamachi, or yellowtail, is mild and clean, perfect for this light starter.

Ingredients:

1 cup peeled, cored, and roughly chopped apples

½ jalapeño, seeded and sliced

¼ cup white wine

¼ cup water

1 teaspoon sugar

½ cup cilantro leaves, packed

1 clove garlic, chopped

½-inch piece ginger, grated

2 tablespoons lime juice (about 1 lime)

¼ cup grapeseed oil

¼ teaspoon salt

8 ounces sushi-grade hamachi (yellowtail)

Mache

8 seedless grapes, halved

Procedure:

1. In a small saucepan over medium heat, combine the apples, jalapeño, wine, water, and sugar and bring to a simmer. Simmer until the apples are very tender when pierced with a knife, about 10 minutes.

2. Meanwhile, in a blender or food processor, combine the cilantro, garlic, ginger, lime juice, oil, and salt, and puree until smooth. Pour the mixture into a small bowl and set aside.

3. Turn the apple mixture into a clean blender or food processor and puree until smooth. Pour into a bowl and refrigerate until needed.

4. Cut the fish into ¼-inch-thick slices.

5. To plate, place a spoonful of the apple puree in the center of each plate and smooth out with the back of the spoon into a circle 2 to 2½ inches in diameter. Arrange the slices of hamachi in a circle on the plates (like the spokes of a wheel). Sprinkle a small handful of the mache over the fish and drizzle with the cilantro vinaigrette. Place a few grapes around the plate and serve.

Serves 4

One can go either way with tartares: assertive flavors or subtle ones that remain in the background, a foil for the fresh fish. We like the clean snapper flavor, but also that of a strong apple, so we suggest a sweet-tart variety, though not one that's too acidic and spicy. Usually for tartares we dice the fish, as it maintains texture. However, for this dish the scraped fish holds the napoleon together. It's a quick, easy way to prepare raw fish: a spoon effortlessly pulls the flesh off the skin. Sushi chefs use this method for spicy tuna rolls and other such preparations. We use an apple corer, a rare event. To present less elaborately, fan thin apple wedges alongside a roughly plated mound of the tartare and garnish with some finely diced apple.

Ingredients:

1¼ pounds red snapper fillet

1½ tablespoons minced cilantro

1 tablespoon mayonnaise

½ tablespoon minced scallion, white and light
    green part only

1½ teaspoons sambal, sriracha, or hot sauce

½ teaspoon salt

¼ teaspoon sesame oil

2 apples, unpeeled

Zest of one lime

Ginger sauce (see sidebar)

Procedure:

1. Using a spoon, scrape the flesh of the snapper from the skin (see headnote) and place in a medium-size bowl. Fold in the remaining ingredients except for the apple, lime zest, and ginger sauce.

2. Peel the apples. With an apple corer, core the apples. Using a mandoline, thinly slice cross-wise into rounds, about ¹⁄₁₆ inch thick. With a 2½-inch ring mold, punch out slices of equal diameter.

3. Place one slice in the center of a cold plate. Set the mold over it. Spoon 1 tablespoon of the tartare onto the apple slice, top with another slice and repeat twice more, ending with apple. Press firmly down with your fingers so the tartare spreads evenly between each layer. Top with one final tablespoon of tartare, gently spreading to form an even layer. Press lightly and remove mold. Repeat with remaining plates.

4. Sprinkle each with a pinch of zest. Drizzle ½ tablespoon of the sauce around each plate and serve.

Serves: 4

Ginger Sauce

2 tablespoons soy sauce

2 teaspoons honey

1½ teaspoons ginger juice

2 tablespoons vegetable oil

1½ tablespoons finely diced cucumber

1½ tablespoons finely diced shallot

2 teaspoons lime juice

Combine the first three ingredients in a small bowl then whisk in the oil. Stir in the remaining three ingredients.

Ginger Juice

Peel an inch-long piece of ginger and grate (preferably on a microplane), then squeeze the juice into a small bowl.

LEMONGRASS SHRIMP WITH MINTED APPLES

Here is a classic Vietnamese snack: marinated shrimp, served with lettuce, a handful of mint and cilantro, and a few dipping sauces. The Vietnamese are famous for balancing the four major taste sensations: sweet, salty, bitter, and sour. With this dish, they do so using only a few ingredients. You don't have to wipe off all the marinade from the shrimp, but because you want the shrimp to sear rather than steam, you should pat them dry. Two pans of very hot oil further ensure a nice sear. That said, the shrimp will still be very tasty if they are cooked in one hot pan. The apple provides crunch; a sweet apple works best with the salt.

Ingredients:

1 stalk lemongrass, white only, chopped

3 inches ginger, peeled and chopped

3 cloves garlic, chopped

1 shallot, chopped

1 cup canola oil

2 teaspoons sugar

1 teaspoon fish sauce or salt

1 teaspoon crushed red pepper flakes

1 pound peeled shrimp

Salt and pepper

4 tablespoons olive oil

1 apple, unpeeled

1 tablespoon fish sauce or rice vinegar

1 bunch mint, rinsed

1 bunch cilantro, rinsed

2 heads Bibb lettuce, washed, leaves separated

Procedure:

1. Combine the first eight ingredients in a blender and pulse until smooth. Place the shrimp in a small bowl and cover with the marinade. Cover with plastic, refrigerate, and let sit for up to 4 hours.

2. Remove the shrimp, drain, and pat dry. Season with salt and pepper. Divide the olive oil between two medium sauté pans and place over high heat until nearly smoking. Divide the shrimp among the pans in one layer (see headnote). Sauté for 2 minutes per side and remove from heat.

3. Peel the apple and julienne finely. To serve, toss the peeled apples with the fish sauce or rice vinegar in a small bowl. Arrange the mint and cilantro on a platter with the lettuce leaves. Place the shrimp in a medium bowl. Lay out the bowls and platter.

4. To compose, place a shrimp and a pinch of apples in each lettuce leaf. Pick off some mint and cilantro leaves, add to the filling, and roll.

Serves 4

"BORSCHT" GRAVLAX

Of all cured items, gravlax is Phil's favorite. It's salty and sweet, but not overbearingly so. It's both lean and unctuous and the best paper-thin food you'll ever eat. It also looks great: You slice through its arrestingly bright green blanket of dill (the traditional cure) to reveal an equally brilliant, rich salmon color. Our gravlax employs a similar Technicolor effect, though the exterior is a deep crimson, caused by beet juice. Try this with a sweet-tart or even a tart apple, which can perform the same function as capers or lemon juice, which often accompany gravlax.

Ingredients:

1½ cups sugar

¾ cup salt

1½ pounds salmon fillet, skin on

2 medium beets, juiced

1½ cups peeled apples, julienned

3 tablespoons sour cream

1 teaspoon horseradish

1 tablespoon lemon juice

½ teaspoon salt

Pumpernickel bread, thinly sliced and toasted

Chive cream cheese

Procedure:

1. In a small bowl combine the sugar and salt. Transfer half the mixture to a small pan just large enough to hold the salmon fillet. Lay the salmon on top, skin side down. Pack the top (flesh side) and sides of the fish with the remaining mixture. Wrap the pan with plastic and refrigerate. Let the fish cure for 48 hours.

2. Rinse the salmon well under running water. Place the salmon back in the pan and pour the beet juice over the fish. Roll the fish in the juice until fully coated, and refrigerate, covered, overnight.

3. For the salad: combine the apples, sour cream, horseradish, lemon juice, and salt.

4. To serve, line ⅓ cup salad on each plate. Shingle four thin slices of gravlax on top of the salad. Quarter the pumpernickel to form toast points and spread with the cream cheese. Serve.

Serves 4

ROASTED MARROW BONE WITH WARM APPLES

Fergus Henderson's London restaurant, St. John, is warm and inviting, both in decor and food. Chef Henderson is well known for cooking with offal, whole pig heads, and so forth, but his deceptively simple marrow bone dish, paired with a parsley-shallot salad, is oft-imitated. Melting and fatty, bone marrow should be in every cookbook. It tastes kind of like the best molten fat off the best steak ever. You don't want to muddy that taste, so a mild, sweet apple works well. Smear the marrow onto the toast, sprinkle with a little salt, and drape an apple slice over the top.

Ingredients:

4 marrow bones

1 large Portuguese roll or baguette

1 tablespoon unsalted butter

2 cups apples, peeled, halved, cored, and
    cut into ¼-inch slices

2 teaspoons finely chopped picholine olives

Salt and pepper

Procedure:

1. Preheat oven to 450°F.

2. Place the bones in a medium sauté pan. Roast in the oven until the marrow is soft and browned, about 20 minutes. (The marrow should not be melted inside but should have some texture when you break into it with a spoon.)

3. Meanwhile, cut the roll into 4 slices, each ¼ inch thick. Cut each slice in half widthwise and toast in the oven. (Or toast 8 slices, each ¼ inch thick, from a baguette.)

4. Melt the butter in a medium sauté pan over medium heat. Add the apples and cook, stirring, until tender. Remove from heat and gently toss with the olives.

5. To serve, place a marrow bone on each plate, along with the toasts and apple/olive salad. If there is fat in the pan that has melted off the bones, spoon it over the bread. Place a small bowl of salt on the table.

Serves 4

There are two types of people: those who like chicken liver and those who don't. We love it sautéed and fried, but it attains heavenly status in the oniony, coarsely textured chopped liver at Barney Greengrass, the Upper West Side institution. Chicken liver mousse is creamy and smooth and a bit more elegant. The sweet-and-sour apples will last a few days in the refrigerator. You can spread this on toast points and lay them out as an hors d'oeuvre, or spoon into a crock alongside a basket of toasts and let your guests go at it. To make this an appetizer, serve in individual ramekins along with some crusty bread and the apples.

Ingredients:

1 pound chicken livers, trimmed of sinew and dried well

Salt and pepper

6 tablespoons olive oil, plus more to cover the mousse

1 cup peeled, cored, and chopped apples

1 cup thinly sliced onion

1 clove garlic, chopped

3 tablespoons cider vinegar

1 cup heavy cream

1 teaspoon ground allspice

1 recipe sweet-and-sour apples (page 142)

Procedure:

1. Pat the livers dry and season on both sides with salt and pepper. Heat 3 tablespoons olive oil in a large sauté pan over medium-high heat. When the oil shimmers, place the livers in a single layer in the pan and brown on all sides, about 2½ minutes per side. Remove from heat and transfer to a blender or food processor.

2. Heat the remaining 3 tablespoons olive oil in the pan over medium-high heat. Add the apples, onions, and garlic and cook until soft and lightly colored, about 5 minutes. Raise the heat and deglaze the pan with the cider vinegar until evaporated. Make sure to scrape the bottom and sides of the pan with a wooden spoon. Transfer the apple mixture to the blender or the food processor containing the livers.

3. Puree the liver-apple mixture with the cream and allspice until smooth. Season to taste with salt and pepper.

4. Transfer the mousse into a glass or plastic container. Slowly pour enough olive oil over the mousse to just cover the top. Cover the container and let cool before refrigerating. Remove from the refrigerator ½ hour before serving.

Yield: 2 cups

PAN-SEARED *FOIE GRAS* WITH POMEGRANATE-APPLE VINAIGRETTE

Foie gras is pricey. And unlike a pork chop, it's not sold by the slice. You have to buy the whole thing (or lobe, in this case). Wait for an occasion; it's worth it. It's easy to cook and as rewarding as anything you'll ever eat.

Ingredients:

1 duck *foie gras,* chilled (about 1½ pounds)

Salt and pepper

1 recipe pomegranate-apple vinaigrette (page 146)

1 recipe cider nuts (page 31)

Procedure:

1. Separate the liver into two lobes and slice into 1-inch medallions, about 4 ounces each. (Heating your knife under hot water makes it easier to cut.) Score each medallion in a diamond pattern and season both sides with salt and pepper.

2. Line a baking tray with paper towels. Heat a large pan over high heat, and sear the *foie gras* for 30 seconds on each side. Remove to prepared tray to drain.

3. To plate: Center the foie gras on each plate, spoon a small pool of the vinaigrette to one side, and a few cider nuts on the other. Serve.

Serves 6

{ HAVE YOU EVER TASTED A REAL APPLE? }

*"Apples are like people. You see, what to me is a dry apple
might not be dry to you. They're all different."*

—Ray Seymour, One of a Kind Apples,
Ithaca, New York

Of the 14,000 apple varieties that grew from the seeds brought here by the English settlers, a mere eleven make up 90 percent of the U.S. apple market. Most Americans can tick off by name the apples sold in their local store: Granny Smith, Fuji, Gala, McIntosh, Red Delicious, and so on. Others, such as Honeycrisp, Macoun, and Empire, may be slightly less familiar but widely available in season. The remaining 10 percent is sold in season at greenmarkets and roadside stands or pick-your-own orchards.

This whittling down of options is not surprising. In fact, it is supremely human. We gravitate toward the comfortable, the familiar, and the predictable. We know they will taste sweet, feel marble-smooth, and come in crayon-like reds, greens, and yellows.

Like any businesspeople, commercial apple growers follow public tastes. However, it is no simple feat to manufacture a sweet, perfect apple, hence the unvarying selection of supermarket apples. While there's nothing wrong with a supermarket apple, it's like watching a game on television versus sitting in the front row.

Lee Calhoun, who, on his two-acre plot in southeastern Georgia, grows over 300 types of Southern antique apples, sums up the American apple market with a shrug: "Americans go to the store and they want three things: a sweet apple, a perfect apple, and a large apple, and commercial orcharding has evolved to give people just that."

Ray Seymour lives in a simple ranch house off a county road, a tan pickup in the driveway. Out back, with its plastic buckets, overspilling bags of soil, ladders, and scattered tools, this could be the home of a weekend gardener. But Seymour's backyard is an archive, a set of stacks deep in the bowels of a university library.

Here, on his few acres, he grows hundreds of antique apple varieties. For decades, he has collected the rootstocks for these trees and nurtured them to fruition. He is part apple grower, part detective: Once he heard that someone had wood from a tree of Carter's Blue (Alabama, 1840), an apple that was, for a while, extinct in the United States. For years, he begged and finally received the rootstock, and so now he has Carter's Blue apples (red with a faint blue flesh) growing behind the house.

Retired, he still goes out back with his wife, and they have a family apple tasting at the kitchen table. Sitting on his couch, he summons tastes, textures, and perfumes.

On the Sheep's Nose (United Kingdom, 1951): "a hard, hard, hard apple. People come to me for it and I say, 'Gosh, you go to your dentist all the time, don't you?' Gosh, it's hard . . . you bite down onto it, it's a bear to get started but it's a beautiful apple, a dark, dark, dark red, polishes up real nice, they call it the mother, the showiest apple in the orchard, green on the inside with black seeds when it's ripe."

On the Fameuse/Snow Apple (France, 1750): "a smaller apple, pure white on the inside, a sweet apple, very tasty."

On the Westfield-Seek-No-Further (Massachusetts, 1700s): "not really a tart apple, a tangy apple. It's got some of that 'you know you've bitten into it taste.' Not really pretty, but I like a hardy finishing apple, and it's got a unique flavor."

Seymour used to haul sacks of apples to the local seniors' center ("we removed the skin—their teeth aren't always that great") and held apple tastings. These were lively evenings, for an apple strikes each palate differently.

"Apples are like people. You see, what to me is a dry apple might not be dry to you. They're all different."

MEAT AND POULTRY

FRIED CHICKEN BASKET WITH CIDER AIOLI 66

OUR HOME ROAST CHICKEN 68

PORK PICCATA 69

SALPICON 70

CIDER RIBS 71

CHOUCROUTE GARNI 72

CRISP PORK BELLY WITH LENTILS AND APPLESAUCE 73

MISO- AND APPLE-MARINATED HANGAR STEAK 74

CIDER-BRAISED SHORT RIBS 76

CALVES' LIVER WITH CIDER-BACON VINAIGRETTE 79

FRIED CHICKEN BASKET WITH CIDER AIOLI

Deboning chicken thighs is the only thorny element of this recipe, but fried chicken is soul food, so why not get your hands dirty? This dish is an example of culturally complementary cooking. Fried chicken and apple pie are two American classics, often served at the same meal, so it makes sense to fiddle around and think of other ways to integrate fried chicken and apples. Hence, the cider aioli and apple butter.

Ingredients:

16 chicken thighs

16 chicken wings

16 chicken livers

Canola oil for frying

3 cups flour

4 cups buttermilk

Salt

1 recipe cider aioli (page 144)

1 recipe apple butter (page 136)

Procedure:

1. Preheat the oven to 200°F.

2. Rinse the chicken pieces and pat dry with paper towels.

3. Prepare the thighs: Hold the end of one thighbone, and with a sharp knife slice around the bone to release the meat. Scrape with the back of your knife down the bone, cutting through any connecting tendons, until you can twist it loose. Repeat.

4. Prepare the wings: Using a chef's knife, cut off and discard the third joint (tip). Cut the remaining two joints in half so the wing is in two pieces. Repeat.

5. Clean the livers: Gently remove as much of the sinew as possible. Cut the large ones in half.

6. Heat 4 inches of canola oil in a large pot to 350°F. Line a tray with paper towels and have another ready.

7. Place the flour in a 9-inch baking dish and the buttermilk in a large bowl. Dunk the chicken thighs in the buttermilk with your left hand, about 4 at a time. Transfer the thighs to the flour and, with your right hand, shake the pan

to coat. Lift the pieces, shaking off any excess flour, and gently place them in the hot oil.

8. Fry until the thighs are cooked through and golden brown, about 6 minutes. Remove the chicken to prepared tray and season immediately with salt. Remove to tray and keep warm in oven. Repeat with the remaining thighs, then the chicken wings and livers, draining on a prepared tray, seasoning with salt, and warming in the oven. The wings should take 4 to 5 minutes and the livers 3 minutes.

9. Serve in a basket alongside the cider aioli and apple butter.

Serves 8

On its own not an apple recipe, but the chicken goes perfectly with twice-baked apple sweet potatoes (page 110). We make this just about once a week, and it never fails. The moment we pull this crispy, moist bird from the oven, our apartment fills with a wonderfully warm fragrance that draws even our two-year-old to the counter, where it rests, the juices settling, waiting to be sliced and served. The secret to a good roast chicken is seasoning well and not opening the oven. Put it in, don't look at it; read a book and let it cook to perfection. You don't have to make a fancy truss; just tie the legs. We don't even bother to tuck back the wing tips, which become deliciously charred and crunchy.

Ingredients:

1 chicken, 3–4 pounds

2 tablespoons chopped thyme

Salt and pepper

Procedure:

1. Preheat oven to 450°F.

2. Liberally season the chicken and cavity with salt and pepper. Lay the bird on its back in a roasting pan. Using butcher's twine, tie drumstick ends together. Roast for 50 minutes.

3. Remove the pan and tilt to collect the fat in one corner. Add the chopped thyme, which will fry in the hot fat. Use a spoon to baste the chicken and let rest for 20 minutes.

4. Make a slice where the legs meet the body and wiggle them loose; find the knuckle, and cut the legs free. Make a smooth slice down one side of the breastbone, trying to stay as close to the bone as possible so as not to lose any meat. Angle the blade to the side of the wishbone and slice off the breast. This takes practice, but pretty soon it'll be a snap.

5. If making chicken for two, serve each person a leg and breast. Otherwise, cut the breasts in half and separate the thighs and drumsticks (or cook another chicken!).

Serves 2–4

Veal pounded thin, floured lightly, sautéed, and served in a lemony butter sauce.

Ingredients:

4 boneless center-cut pork chops,
    6–8 ounces each

Salt and pepper

½ cup flour

¼ cup olive oil

1 large endive

½ English cucumber

2 apples, unpeeled

2 heads radicchio, torn into bite-size pieces

½ red onion, thinly sliced

¼ cup sherry vinaigrette (see sidebar)

Procedure:

1. Place a chop between two pieces of plastic wrap and, using a meat mallet or rolling pin, pound the cutlets until they are ¼ inch thick. Set aside and repeat with the remaining chops.

2. Season the cutlets with salt and pepper and dredge in the flour, shaking off any excess. Heat oil in a large sauté pan over high heat. When shimmering, add the cutlets and cook until brown, about 1 minute. Flip and cook 1 more minute. Keep warm by covering loosely with foil.

3. Trim the bottom of the endive and peel off the leaves. Slice lengthwise into thin matchsticks. Cut the cucumber in half. Reserve one half for another use. Peel, halve lengthwise and remove seeds with a spoon. Slice into thin half-moons. Add to a large bowl.

4. Cut the apple into ¼-inch dice, add to the bowl along with the onions and toss with the vinaigrette. Season.

5. To serve, top each pork chop with a heaping portion of salad.

Serves 2–4

Sherry Vinaigrette

¼ cup sherry vinegar

1 teaspoon minced shallot

¼ teaspoon Dijon mustard

¾ cup olive oil

Salt and pepper

Combine vinegar, shallots, and mustard in a medium bowl and whisk. Slowly add the oil in a thin stream, whisking constantly. Season with salt and pepper.

Yield: 1 cup

SALPICON

Our friend Mike Nannizzi is a hard-core backyard griller. Anything that can be smoked and grilled, he's done it: beer-can chickens, rib roasts, pork shoulders, briskets, even offal. Mike's parents are from Guatemala, where locals serve salpicon, a dish of braised pork rolled in a tortilla with lemon and some simple raw vegetables. Try to use a whole piece of pork shoulder rather than cubes. A single cut will cook longer and develop a great, clean flavor. A tart or sweet-tart apple works well, boosting the pork with some acid.

Ingredients:

2 tablespoons chili powder

2 tablespoons dried oregano

¼ teaspoon ground cloves

1 tablespoon salt

¼ cup canola oil

1½ pounds pork shoulder

3 cups apple cider

1 tablespoon minced chipotle in adobo

4 large flour tortillas

2 apples, unpeeled

1 bunch radishes, washed

1 tablespoon lemon juice

2 tablespoons olive oil

Salt and pepper

Procedure:

1. Preheat oven to 350°F.

2. Mix the first four ingredients in a small bowl and massage into the pork shoulder.

3. In a large pot over medium-high heat, heat canola oil until shimmering. Carefully add the pork and brown on all sides, 8 to 10 minutes. Pour in the cider and bring to a boil over high heat. Cover and cook in the oven until very tender, 2 to 2½ hours. Remove and let cool in the braising liquid. Reduce the oven to 200°F.

4. When the pork has cooled, remove the meat from the liquid and shred into a bowl. Return the braising liquid to the stove and reduce over medium-high heat by half. Add the pork and chipotle to the liquid to heat through. Remove from heat.

5. Wrap the tortillas in foil and warm in the oven.

6. Peel, halve, core, quarter, and use a mandoline to slice the apples thinly. Slice the radish thinly, ⅛ inch thick. Toss with the lemon juice and olive oil and season with salt and pepper.

7. To serve, pile some pork down the middle of the tortilla, top with the apple salad, and roll.

Serves 4

Phil and I don't like a lot of sauce all over our ribs, just a coating of dry rub and a sharp vinegar sauce on the side. As city dwellers, we've cooked these in the oven with excellent results, slow-cooking in foil and then broiling at the last minute to simulate the grill, but it just reminds Phil of our yardless life. Serve with the cider vinegar barbecue sauce (page 148).

Ingredients:

2 racks spare ribs, about 5 pounds each

4 quarts apple juice

½ recipe rub (see sidebar)

2 cups cider

1 recipe cider vinegar barbecue sauce

Procedure:

1. Place the ribs meat side down in deep pans (use two if necessary), pour over the apple juice (it doesn't have to be completely submerged), cover, and refrigerate overnight.

2. Remove the ribs, dry well with paper towels, and massage the rub liberally over both sides. Place on trays, wrap with plastic wrap, and refrigerate up to 6 hours.

3. Cook the ribs over indirect heat: If using a gas grill, light half the burners and place the ribs over the other half. If using a charcoal grill, heat the coals and rake the hot coals to opposite sides, placing an aluminum drip pan under the grate in the center. Place the racks on the grill over the pan, cover the grill, and cook at 250°F for about 2½ hours, basting every 30 minutes with the cider.

4. The ribs are done when you lift one end and the other flops down. Remove the top of the grill, place directly over the heat, and sear on both sides until browned, even a bit burnt, if you like. Remove, slice, and serve with the cider vinegar barbecue sauce.

Serves 4–6

Rub

8 tablespoons brown sugar

4 tablespoons kosher salt

2 teaspoons garlic powder

2 tablespoons dried oregano

3 tablespoons chili powder

2 tablespoons paprika

1 teaspoon ground cumin

2 tablespoons red pepper flakes

Combine all the ingredients and store in an airtight container. It will keep for several months.

Yield: 1 cup

The makings of a great choucroute lie within a few square blocks of our home. On Sullivan Street, our butcher, Pino, makes all his own sausages and sells the freshest smoked pork chops and slab bacon; on Orchard Street, Guss' brines the best pickles and sauerkraut in town. Actually, unbeknownst to them, most New Yorkers live a hop, skip, and a jump from a humble, makeshift version of this Alsatian classic. Hot dog vendors poach hot dogs in a brackish mix of water and the strained juices from the sauerkraut bag. When you order a "dog with 'kraut," you're getting a pared-down choucroute! Use an apple that will hold its shape, such as a good baking apple.

Ingredients:

½ pound slab bacon, ¼ inch thick, medium diced

4 pork chops, bone-in, about 1 inch thick

2 bratwurst

2 kielbasa

1 large onion, cut into medium-size dice

3 cups peeled, diced apples (½-inch dice)

½ teaspoon caraway seeds

½ teaspoon juniper berries

½ teaspoon cloves

2 bay leaves

2 pounds sauerkraut, drained, brine reserved

2 12-ounce bottles cider beer

1 quart chicken stock (see sidebar, page 51)

½ teaspoon salt

Procedure:

1. In a large pot over medium heat, render bacon until crispy. Remove with a slotted spoon onto a paper towel and set aside. Remove all but 2 tablespoons of the bacon grease and reserve. Over high heat in the same pot, brown the pork chops, bratwurst, and kielbasa in batches. Remove the meats from the pot and set aside.

2. Once the pot has cooled slightly, heat 2 tablespoons of the reserved bacon grease over medium heat. Add the onions and cook until soft and translucent, about 5 to 8 minutes. Add the apples and cook for another 3 minutes, stirring occasionally. Add the spices and bay leaves and stir for 1 minute. Add half of the sauerkraut and stir to combine. Place the pork chops, bratwurst, kielbasa, and bacon back into the pot, and top with the remaining sauerkraut. Add the cider beer, stock, ½ cup of the reserved brine, and salt and bring to a boil. Turn down the heat to simmer for 1½ hours.

3. With a slotted spoon remove the sauerkraut and apple mixture to a platter. Arrange the pork chops, kielbasa, and bratwurst over and around. Serve.

Serves 4

CRISP PORK BELLY WITH LENTILS AND APPLESAUCE

Pork belly is essentially spare ribs stripped of the bones. We've served it many times, and it's deliciously fatty and luscious. We think roasting produces the finest result, as it gives you those wonderful cracklings, but you can braise it or, if you're feeling decadent, braise large cubes, cool them off, and deep-fry. When ready to slice, we flip it over because the cracklings are brittle and require a bit of leverage when slicing.

Ingredients:

4½ teaspoons coriander seeds

1 tablespoon fennel seeds

3 cloves

1½ teaspoons paprika

3 pounds pork belly, rind on

Salt and pepper

2 cups cider

1 recipe cooked lentils (page 41)

1 recipe applesauce (page 134)

Procedure:

1. Preheat oven to 400°F.

2. Add the first three ingredients to a medium pan over medium-heat and toast until fragrant, 2 to 3 minutes. In a spice grinder or mortar and pestle, coarsely grind the toasted spices then stir in the paprika to combine. Reserve in a small bowl.

3. Season the pork on all sides with salt and pepper, then massage with 2 tablespoons of the spice mix. Lay the pork skin side up on a rack in a roasting pan. Place in the oven on the center rack and roast for about 2 hours. The skin should be well browned and crisp. Remove and rest on a rack for 20 minutes.

4. Meanwhile, heat the cider in a medium saucepan over medium-high heat and reduce to ⅓ cup, 10 to 12 minutes. Remove from heat and reserve.

5. Place the roast on a cutting board, brush the cider glaze over the top and bottom, then sprinkle on the remaining spice mix. Flip the roast skin side down and make 1-inch-thick slices. You'll need some elbow grease to cut through the crackling. Serve on top of the lentils and applesauce.

Serves 4–6

MISO- AND APPLE-MARINATED HANGAR STEAK

Because it is sweet and light, Japanese chefs tend to use white miso in fish marinades, while they gravitate to the saltier, more robust brown miso when dealing with meat. Hangar steak, which is a rich cut, calls for brown miso. Don't marinate longer than overnight, as the salty miso will begin to cure the meat. Miso and sugar are buddies; here we substitute the apple's natural sweetness for sugar. The steak goes well with cauliflower-apple puree (page 106) and chimichurri sauce. Use a sweet apple.

Ingredients:

FOR THE MARINADE:

2 tablespoons red miso

¼ teaspoon soy sauce

½ cup apple cider

1 anchovy

Juice of 1 lime

¾ teaspoon Dijon mustard

1½ teaspoons sambal or hot sauce

1 small clove garlic

¼ cup brown sugar

½-inch piece ginger, peeled

3 tablespoons peanut butter

¼ teaspoon fresh black pepper

1 apple, peeled, cored, and chopped

FOR THE STEAK:

2 pounds hangar steak in one piece

Salt and pepper

2 tablespoons olive oil

1 recipe cauliflower-apple puree (page xxx)

½ recipe chimichurri sauce (see sidebar)

Procedure:

1. Preheat oven to 400°F.

2. To prepare the marinade: Puree all the ingredients in a blender or food processor until smooth.

3. Trim the steak: Using a sharp knife, remove the tough center membrane. Trim any scraps to make a neat steak. Divide into even portions. Lightly season the steaks on both sides with salt and pepper.

4. Place the steak in a large baking pan, pour over the marinade, and cover with plastic wrap. Refrigerate for up to 6 hours.

5. Pat steaks dry and season both sides with salt and pepper. Heat the oil in a large sauté pan over high heat, until shimmering. Add the steaks and cook 3 to 4 minutes on each side for medium rare (smaller pieces will take less time). Remove from heat to a platter and let rest 10 minutes.

6. To plate: Place the steak over the cauliflower-apple puree; serve with chimichurri sauce on top or on the side.

Serves 6

Chimichurri

2 cups chopped parsley, leaves only, about 1 bunch

5 garlic cloves, peeled and chopped

¼ cup chopped onion

1 teaspoon red pepper flakes

1 teaspoon dried oregano

¼ cup cider vinegar

1 cup olive oil

Salt and pepper

Add all the ingredients but the salt and pepper to a food processor or blender. Puree until combined but not entirely smooth. The sauce should have some texture. Season with salt and pepper. It will keep in the refrigerator for a few weeks.

Yield: 2 cups

CIDER-BRAISED SHORT RIBS

Every Passover, Phil's mother made tzimmes, an almost candy-sweet stew of sweet potatoes, brown sugar, carrots, and short ribs, which he proceeded to devour over the next twenty-four hours. It was an early introduction to short ribs, the perfect cut for braises. Our tamarind short ribs have, over the years, been our most requested dish. These cider-based ribs are nearly as delicious. The key to great short ribs is selection: You need the meatiest possible. Either have your butcher cut them or select the best the supermarket is offering. Spoon the sauce around the ribs so as not to wash off the glaze, to which the green peppercorns will adhere. Homemade veal or chicken stock will make this—and all braises—special: The stock is richer and, when reduced, creates a full-bodied sauce.

Ingredients:

6 pounds short ribs in single pieces on the bone

Salt and pepper

Olive oil

4 cups red wine

4 cups veal or chicken stock (see recipes, pages 78 and 51)

2 sprigs rosemary

2 tablespoons yellow mustard seeds

2 carrots, peeled and sliced in ½-inch pieces

2 ribs celery, sliced in ½-inch pieces

1 onion, diced in ½-inch pieces

3 cloves garlic, sliced

½ cup calvados

1 cup apple juice

¼ cup soy sauce

½ cup honey

½ bulb fennel, shaved thinly on a mandoline

2 tablespoons green peppercorns, drained

Procedure:

1. Preheat oven to 325°F.

2. Lay the ribs flat on a tray and season well on all sides with salt and pepper.

3. Heat 2 tablespoons olive oil in a large pot over high heat. When the oil shimmers, carefully place some of the ribs in a single layer in the pot to brown on all sides. Don't crowd the pot or the meat won't brown. Remove ribs to a large bowl and repeat until all the meat is well browned, 8 to 10 minutes.

4. Return the meat to the pot along with the wine, stock, rosemary, and mustard seeds.

5. Reduce the heat slightly. Add 2 more tablespoons of olive oil and add the vegetables. Stir frequently until they are well caramelized. Pour in the calvados; be careful, it will sputter greatly. Reduce until nearly dry, scraping any bits from the bottom with a wooden spoon. Bring to a boil, cover, and place in the oven. After about 15 minutes, make sure the liquid isn't boiling (should be at a gentle simmer). If so, turn the oven down a bit. Braise until the meat is very tender, 2 to 2½ hours.

6. Remove the ribs from the braising liquid to a foil-lined baking sheet and cover loosely with foil to keep warm. Using a ladle, skim as much fat as possible from the sauce and strain through a fine mesh strainer into a medium pot. Reduce on high until you have 2 cups.

7. For the glaze: Bring the apple juice, soy sauce, and honey to a boil in a small saucepan and reduce on high heat until syrupy.

8. When ready to serve, preheat the broiler and place a rack 6 inches from the heating source. Brush the ribs with the glaze and place under the broiler until sizzling, 45 seconds to 1 minute.

9. Serve the ribs in bowls; ladle the sauce around, avoiding the glaze. Stand some fennel in the middle of the meat and sprinkle green peppercorns on top of the meat. Serve.

Serves 4

Veal Stock

Making veal stock can be messy, as the bones are roasted at a high heat prior to being simmered, at least the roasting bones smell delicious. You'll probably need a few pots to accommodate the sizable bones.

¼ cup canola oil

10 pounds veal bones (see note)

1 celery rib, chopped

2 large carrots, unpeeled and chopped

2 beefsteak tomatoes, chopped

Large onion, unpeeled and chopped

1 cup water

2 bay leaves

1 tablespoon black peppercorns

2 sprigs thyme

1. Preheat oven to 425°F.

2. Spread the canola oil on a large roasting pan or baking sheet (you may need two). Place in oven for 10 minutes. Remove pan and carefully add bones. They will sizzle. Make sure not to overcrowd by adding too many bones. Return pan to oven. After 45 minutes, turn the bones and scatter the vegetables among them. Continue roasting for another 45 minutes or until the bones are well browned.

3. Place the bones in a large pot on the stove and reserve the vegetables in a separate bowl.

4. Wearing oven mitts, carefully place the roasting pan or baking sheet over a burner at medium heat. Add the water and, using a wooden spoon, deglaze the tray by scraping as many remaining bits as possible. The water should simmer. Carefully pour deglazing liquid into the pot with the bones. Fill the pot with cold water, covering the bones by 2 inches. Add the remaining ingredients. Bring to a boil over medium-high heat. Boil a few minutes, skimming the scum from the top. Turn the heat to low and let simmer for at least 8 hours. With 1 hour to go, add the reserved vegetables.

5. When done, strain through a fine mesh strainer (chinois) into a large pot. Boil the stock until reduced by about a third.

6. Let stock cool to room temperature and refrigerate overnight. Skim off any fat that has solidified at the top and pour the stock into plastic containers. It will last 4 days in the refrigerator or 4 months in the freezer.

Yield: 4 quarts

CALVES' LIVER WITH CIDER-BACON VINAIGRETTE

Calves' liver should be medium rare to medium, pink and creamy on the inside. Cooked any longer, it becomes dry and gamey. Slab bacon is the best accompaniment as it can be sliced thickly, which is more appropriate for an entree than the packaged variety.

Ingredients:

½ pound slab bacon, sliced ⅛ inch thick

½ cup cider

¾ cup olive oil

2 tablespoons cider vinegar

1 teaspoon Dijon mustard

2 tablespoons minced chives

Salt and pepper

1½ pounds calves' liver, sliced ½ inch thick

½ cup flour

8 sage leaves

2 tablespoons unsalted butter

Procedure:

1. Preheat oven to 400°F.

2. Lay the bacon slices on a baking sheet and roast in oven until crisp, 15 to 20 minutes. Remove bacon to a paper-towel-lined plate and pour the bacon fat into a small bowl.

3. Meanwhile, bring the cider to a boil in a small saucepan over high heat, and reduce to 2 tablespoons, about 6 minutes.

4. In a small bowl, combine 3 tablespoons of the reserved bacon fat, the reduced cider, ¼ cup of the olive oil, cider vinegar, and mustard. Whisk to emulsify. Fold in chives and season with salt and pepper.

5. Divide the remaining ½ cup olive oil between two large sauté pans over high heat. Season the liver slices on both sides with salt and pepper, and dredge in the flour. When the oil is shimmering, lift and shake off any excess flour from the liver and carefully add 2 to each pan.

6. Sauté until browned and crispy on the bottom, about 2 minutes, then flip and add the sage leaves and 1 tablespoon of butter to each pan. Tilting the pan, baste liver with the butter, and sauté for another 2 minutes. It should be pink inside. If you like it medium rare, cook another minute.

7. Remove to 4 plates, drizzle with some vinaigrette, and crisscross 2 slices of bacon on top. Serve.

Serves 4

 FISH

SALMON BURGER WITH APPLE CORN SLAW 82

SEARED TUNA WITH PARSLEY AND APPLE-CAPER RELISH 83

SQUID WITH BROWN BUTTER SAUCE 84

SCALLOPS WITH GREEN APPLE NAGE 85

ROAST SNAPPER WITH CHORIZO 86

SEAFOOD SAUSAGE WITH APPLE-FENNEL SALAD 88

CLAM CASSOULET 90

SALMON BURGER WITH APPLE CORN SLAW

Burgers inspire heated arguments. Some like a hefty patty where the juice runs down your arm. Others prefer a moist but more manageable package. A properly done salmon burger is a good meat substitute, and cooked to medium rare, it straddles the line: It's both moist and meaty, but not dripping with juice. A tart apple is perfect as it cuts the fatty salmon and the sweet corn.

Ingredients:

4 tablespoons olive oil

2 pounds salmon, skin and bones removed

1 tablespoon minced shallot

¼ cup chopped parsley

1 cup fresh breadcrumbs

1 egg, beaten

Salt and pepper

4 hamburger rolls, split and toasted

1 recipe apple corn slaw

Procedure:

1. Line a baking sheet with foil and spread with 2 tablespoons of the olive oil. Chop salmon finely with a knife. In a large bowl, combine the salmon, shallot, parsley, breadcrumbs, and egg, and salt and pepper to taste. Fold together to combine, but don't overmix. Form patties about 3 inches wide and 1 inch thick. Refrigerate on prepared sheet pan for at least 1 hour. Meanwhile, prepare apple corn slaw.

2. Heat the remaining oil in a large sauté pan over medium-high heat. When oil shimmers, add the patties and cook 3 minutes per side.

3. Top bun with burger, then slaw and serve.

Serves 4

Apple Corn Slaw

1 cup peeled and finely julienned apples

1 ear corn

3 tablespoons mayonnaise

1 teaspoon cider vinegar

Salt and pepper

Place apples in a small bowl. Stand the corn upright and cut off the kernels. Place in the bowl. Using the back of the knife, scrape down the cob to extract its "milk," the sweet juice inside. Add the mayonnaise and cider vinegar to the bowl and season with salt and pepper.

SEARED TUNA WITH PARSLEY AND APPLE-CAPER RELISH

Phil's never been a huge tuna sandwich guy. In his opinion, tuna is best when treated like a steak: seasoned well with salt and pepper and charred over a hot fire. As with a steak, the joy lies In the contrast between a firm, pleasantly charred exterior and a silky, lean interior. He likes thick, meaty steaks, hence our recipe, which calls for large 10-ounce pieces. To serve, slice each steak against the grain in offbeat chunks (some on the bias, some not), and arrange neatly.

Ingredients:

3 tuna steaks, each about 10 ounces and 1½ inches thick

Salt and pepper

¼ cup plus 2 tablespoons olive oil

2 cups peeled, diced sweet-tart apple (¼-inch dice)

1 cup minced parsley

3 tablespoons chopped capers

1 shallot, minced

½ lemon, juiced

Procedure:

1. Season the tuna on both sides with salt and pepper. Heat 2 tablespoons of the oil in a large sauté pan over high heat. When almost smoking, add the tuna and cook 2 minutes per side. Remove to a platter.

2. In a small bowl, toss the apple, parsley, capers, and shallot. Mix with the lemon juice and remaining olive oil. Season with salt and pepper.

3. Slice the tuna steaks (see headnote). Arrange on plates and spoon the relish over.

Serves 4

SQUID WITH BROWN BUTTER SAUCE

Our version of skate with brown butter sauce, this is one of those recipes in which the apple, tossed in at the last minute, plays a supporting yet integral role. A tart apple is great for this: It cuts through the rich butter and the sweet squid.

Ingredients:

2 pounds squid, cleaned

Salt and pepper

4 tablespoons olive oil

8 tablespoons unsalted butter

1 cup black raisins

1 cup cooked chickpeas, cut in half

1 cup peeled and diced apples (¼-inch dice)

Juice of 1 lemon

2 tablespoons minced parsley

¼ cup peeled and finely julienned apples

Procedure:

1. Slice open the squid bodies, rinse off any grit, and slice widthwise in ¼-inch by 2-inch strips. Slice the tentacles in half, lay the squid on a tray, and dry well. Season with salt and pepper.

2. Heat the oil in a large sauté pan over high heat. When shimmering, add the squid and sauté for 1 to 2 minutes, until opaque. (Be careful not to overcook, or it becomes rubbery.) Remove pan from heat and drain squid in a colander.

3. Empty any oil or liquid from the pan, and wipe clean with a paper towel. Add the butter, and place over medium-high heat. When butter browns, about 1 minute, add the raisins, chickpeas, and apple. Cook until the chickpeas fry, 1 more minute. Remove from heat and stir in 1 tablespoon of the lemon juice and parsley.

4. Divide the squid among 4 plates. Spoon the butter sauce and any remaining lemon juice over each serving. Top with a small pile of the julienned apple and serve.

Serves 4

SCALLOPS WITH GREEN APPLE NAGE

Here, and in the green apple gelato (page 128), vitamin C powder comes into play. It's available at health food stores, lasts a long time, and prevents apples and apple juice from turning brown. In French, *nage* means bath. It is a subtle broth of wine, vinegar, herbs, and spices, usually used to poach fish, but it can be interpreted loosely.

Ingredients:

3 Granny Smith apples, unpeeled and cut in chunks

½ teaspoon vitamin C powder

2 cups parsnips in 1-inch chunks

2½ cups milk

Salt and pepper

16 sea scallops

4 tablespoons olive oil

4 tablespoons unsalted butter

Procedure:

1. Pass the apple chunks through a juicer, skim the foam, and stir in the vitamin C powder. Reserve.

2. Combine the parsnips and milk in a small saucepan, bring to a simmer over medium-high heat, and cook until tender, 10 to 15 minutes. Puree the parsnips with some of the milk in a blender or food processor until smooth. Season with salt and pepper.

3. Season the scallops on both sides with salt and pepper. Divide the oil and butter between 2 large sauté pans over high heat. When the foam begins to subside, add the scallops and cook until well colored, 2½ to 3 minutes on each side.

4. To finish, spoon 3 tablespoons of parsnips in the center of a soup bowl. Use it as a bed for 4 scallops and pour 3 tablespoons of the nage around. Repeat with the remaining scallops and serve.

Serves 4

ROAST SNAPPER WITH CHORIZO

Whole fish, roasted or grilled, is an awesome thing and the best way to cook and eat fish. The meat is fragrant from the herbs and lemon, and it doesn't dry out. A whole fish also appeals to the carnivore, who can pick clean every last bone. Cider-braised chorizo gives it a Spanish flair and a sauce thin enough to seep into the flaked flesh. We've left out the amount of olive oil deliberately: We like the dish generously oiled, but you may prefer less. For individual portions, use smaller fish such as dorade and branzino. They will take about 10 minutes to cook.

Ingredients:

½ cup chopped dill

½ cup chopped parsley

3 cloves garlic, chopped

Olive oil (see headnote)

Salt and pepper

3–4 pound snapper, scaled and cleaned

2 lemons, cut in ⅛-inch slices

1 bulb fennel, sliced to ⅛ inch on mandoline

2 bunches scallions

1 recipe cider-braised chorizo (see sidebar)

Procedure:

1. Preheat oven to 425°F.

2. Toss the herbs and garlic in a bowl with olive oil and season with salt and pepper.

3. On a large cutting board or baking sheet, rub the fish all over with olive oil. Season the entire fish, including the cavity, with salt and pepper. Stuff the cavity with ⅔ of the herb mixture and shingle 3 lemon slices on top of the herbs.

4. Drizzle about ¼ cup of olive oil down the center of another baking sheet. Lay the fennel in a line over the oil roughly the length of the fish. Drizzle the fennel with olive oil and season with salt and pepper. Top with the rest of the herbs and lemon slices. Set the fish on top. In a medium bowl, toss the scallions with some olive oil, season lightly with salt and pepper, and scatter over and around the fish, tucking some underneath. Roast in the oven for 35 to 40 minutes.

5. To serve, set out four deep bowls. Using two large spoons lift the fish in boneless chunks and divide among the bowls. Spoon the cider-braised chorizo around and top with fennel and scallions.

Serves 4–6

Cider-braised Chorizo

10 ounces chorizo, cut in ¼-inch slices

1 cup cider

Brown chorizo in a small saucepan until some fat renders and it is lightly colored. Add cider and reduce over low heat, about ½ hour or until the broth is a rich copper color.

SEAFOOD SAUSAGE WITH APPLE-FENNEL SALAD

We live near Little Italy, site of the annual Feast of San Gennaro. Streets are blocked off and lined with carny guess-your-weight stands and funnel cake fryers. To us, these are merely a distraction from the sausage-and-pepper guys with their massive, spicy-sweet subs. Sausages need not be in a sub; they can be more refined, a combination of seafood and herbs, crisped under the broiler and served with a refreshing fennel/apple salad. These can be frozen: poach, cool, then wrap tightly in plastic and aluminum foil. When ready to use, defrost, halve, and broil.

Ingredients:

¾ pound shrimp, peeled

¾ pound sea scallops

½ pound cod

Juice 2 limes

1 tablespoon cider vinegar

½ cup canola oil

3 garlic cloves, minced

1 jalapeño, sliced

¾ cup chopped parsley

Salt and pepper

¼ cup olive oil

1 recipe apple-fennel salad (see sidebar)

Procedure:

1. Place the seafood, lime juice, cider vinegar, ½ cup of the oil, garlic, jalapeño, and parsley in a food processor and pulse until smooth. Season well with salt and pepper. Test the seasoning by frying a small spoonful of the mix. Adjust as desired.

2. With a rubber spatula, scoop the mixture into a heavy ziplock bag. Cut a 1½-inch hole from one of the corners. (Or use a piping bag.)

3. On your cutting board or other flat surface, lay a sheet of plastic wrap 12 inches long. Pipe a sausage 1½ inches wide and 6 inches long down the center of the plastic. Twist the ends tightly to compress and form a sausage shape. It's okay if they come out slightly different sizes. It takes a bit of practice. Refrigerate.

4. Bring a large pot of water to a simmer over medium-high heat. Fill a large bowl with ice water and place next to stove. Drop sausages into the pot and poach for 6 to 8 minutes. Using a slotted spoon, remove to ice bath. When cool, remove to a plate or platter and refrigerate for 30 minutes. Meanwhile, prepare apple-fennel salad.

5. Heat the broiler to high and place a rack 6 inches from the heat source. Coat a baking sheet with 2 tablespoons olive oil. Remove sausages from plastic wrap and split in half lengthwise. Lay them on the baking sheet and drizzle with remaining olive oil. Place on the rack and broil until browned, about 3 minutes. Remove.

6. To serve, on a small plate, arrange two sausage halves, cut side up, in a v-shape. Place a small pile of salad in the center.

Serves 4

Apple-fennel Salad

1 bulb fennel

2 tart apples, unpeeled, halved, cored, and quartered

Juice ½ lemon

2 tablespoons olive oil

Salt and pepper

Using a mandoline, slice the fennel and apples very thinly, ⅛ inch. In a medium bowl, toss with the lemon juice and olive oil, and season with salt and pepper.

CLAM CASSOULET

Baked beans and cider are a loving couple, and the two—to continue the metaphor—are no less happily married here. This dish is a hybrid between true cassoulet—a rich dish of duck confit and beans—and New England clam chowder. We like to keep the clams whole, ensuring a nice, full spoonful of sweet clam. Stir the clams once so they cook evenly, but don't overcook because they will be returned to the hot stew. Also, don't put the beans on and go for a drive: They should be covered with liquid and stirred occasionally.

Ingredients:

2 cups white beans

¾ cup cider

4 sprigs thyme

5 dozen littleneck clams (about 7 pounds), washed well

3 tablespoons unsalted butter

1 medium carrot, peeled, cut into ¼-inch dice

1 celery rib, cut into ¼-inch dice

1 small onion, cut into ¼-inch dice

4 cups chicken stock (see sidebar, page 51)

1 tablespoon cornstarch

½ cup heavy cream

2 tablespoons calvados (optional)

½ cup chopped parsley

Salt and pepper

Procedure:

1. Soak the beans overnight in enough cold water to cover by several inches. Drain well.

2. Bring the cider to a boil in a large pot over high heat. Add 2 thyme sprigs and clams, and cover. Let cook 2 minutes then stir from bottom to top. Replace the cover and steam until open, 6 to 7 minutes total. Remove from heat.

3. When cool enough to handle, pick the clams into a bowl and refrigerate. Discard the shells and strain the broth through a fine mesh strainer. You should have about 3 cups. Reserve.

4. Melt the butter in another large pot over medium heat. Add the vegetables and cook until softened but not colored, stirring frequently, 8 minutes.

5. Add the beans, and stir to combine. Then pour in the chicken stock, clam broth, and the remaining thyme. Simmer gently until the beans are cooked (they should hold their form and be creamy inside), 1½ to 2½ hours. Make sure to stir occasionally so they cook evenly. (If they peek out of the liquid, add a bit of water to keep them submerged.)

6. With a slotted spoon, transfer 2 cups of the cooked beans to a blender. Puree with 1 cup of the cooking liquid until smooth, return to the pot, and stir gently to combine.

7. In a small bowl, dissolve the cornstarch with 1 tablespoon of water and stir into the stew. Fold in the cream, calvados, reserved clams, and parsley. Season with salt and plenty of black pepper. Serve hot.

Serves 4–6

A NOTE ON CIDER VERSUS APPLE JUICE:

Apple cider and apple juice are the product of pressed apples. Apple juice makers, however, strain the liquid and treat it with preservatives, which, among other things, stifle oxidation. They also often add sugar. Cider producers don't strain—hence the muddy dregs at the bottom of the container—and they may or may not add preservatives. We tend to use exclusively cider in our recipes. It is a bit pricier but far richer in apple flavor, especially when reduced to a syrup. To marinate ribs or chicken, we prefer apple juice, which is less expensive and lighter, and doesn't overwhelm the ingredient. Be sure to skim cider when boiling, as it tends to develop a scum on top.

PASTA

MAC 'N CHEESE 94

GNOCCHI WITH CAULIFLOWER, PEAS, AND APPLES 96

APPLE RISOTTO 98

LAMB AND MASCARPONE RAVIOLI 102

MAC 'N CHEESE

On January 4, 2006, Julia Moskin, a food writer for the *New York Times,* wrote a much-discussed and appreciated article about macaroni and cheese. We played around with her idea for cheesy mac 'n cheese, adding apples, pears, an egg, ricotta, and heavy cream. You can use plain applesauce, but we found that a dense puree makes for a smoother result. The recipe yields a cheesy product without the heavy, often floury sauce. We've made this with shredded meat from smoked ham hocks. It's simple: simmer a few hocks in apple juice and water until falling off the bone. Let cool, shred into the pasta, and pop into the oven. Use a sweet apple, which complements the fatty cheese. Enjoy.

Ingredients:

1 tablespoon unsalted butter

1 cup milk

½ cup heavy cream

⅛ teaspoon nutmeg

Pinch cayenne

1 teaspoon ground mustard powder

1 cup ricotta

1 egg

½ teaspoon salt

Black pepper

½ pound elbow macaroni, prepared according to package directions

½ cup apple-pear puree (page 137)

1 pound sharp cheddar, grated (about 2 cups), ¼ cup reserved

Procedure:

1. Preheat the oven to 375°F.

2. Butter a 9-inch square or round baking pan thoroughly.

3. In a blender, puree all the ingredients, except for the macaroni, apple-pear puree, and cheddar. Transfer the blender contents to a large bowl, and mix well with the macaroni, apple-pear puree, and cheese. Pour the mixture into the prepared pan, cover tightly with foil, and bake for ½ hour. Remove the foil, top with the reserved cheese, bake another ½ hour, or until brown and bubbling. Remove and let sit at least 20 minutes.

Serves 4

GNOCCHI WITH CAULIFLOWER, PEAS, AND APPLES

The trick to this, and many pasta recipes, is keeping it simple and having your ingredients at hand, ready to be folded into the pasta. Gnocchi is a delightfully creamy bite, which lends itself to a variety of sauces. Because they are so rich, smaller portions are appropriate, especially when tossed in cream. When pasta absorbs too much of the cream, it will congeal and become gluey, so reserve some of the pasta water and add a few tablespoons to thin it out: There should be a little puddle of sauce at the bottom of the bowl. The cauliflower florets should be small and delicate—not larger than the gnocchi.

Ingredients:

½ cup peas, fresh or frozen, thawed

2 cups cauliflower florets, about ¾ inch (see headnote)

¼ cup pine nuts

1½ cups peeled and diced sweet apples (¼-inch dice)

2 cups heavy cream

½ recipe gnocchi (see sidebar)

½ cup freshly grated Parmesan

Pinch freshly grated nutmeg

Salt and pepper

Procedure:

1. Place a large pot of well-salted water over medium-high heat and bring to a boil. Place a few handfuls of ice in a large bowl and fill with plenty of cold water. Add peas and boil 1 minute if frozen, 3 minutes if fresh. Using a slotted spoon, remove peas to a small bowl, run under cold water. Drain and reserve.

2. Add cauliflower to water and blanch until crisp-tender, 3 minutes. Remove with a slotted spoon, and transfer to ice bath. Drain and reserve.

3. Toast pine nuts in a small sauté pan over medium-low heat, 4 to 5 minutes. Be careful they don't burn. Reserve in a small bowl.

4. Place the apples in a small bowl. Now you have all the elements for the dish, so keep your bowls near the stove.

5. Place a large sauté pan over medium-high heat and add the cream. Bring to a simmer and let reduce by half. Add the cauliflower. Drop the gnocchi in the boiling water. When gnocchi float, 2 to 3 minutes, reserve ½ cup of the pasta water (see headnote). Remove gnocchi with a slotted spoon and add to the pan.

6. Roll in sauce for 1 minute. Add peas, apples, and pine nuts, and fold everything together. Add the Parmesan, nutmeg, salt, and plenty of fresh black pepper and toss well. If the gnocchi absorbs too much of the cream, add a few tablespoons of the water to thin it out. Serve in shallow bowls.

Serves 4–6

Gnocchi

To make fresh gnocchi you don't need any fancy equipment, and you can roll your hands in a bowlful of warm potatoes. While there are many gnocchi recipes, we stick to the 3-2-1 ratio. Not only is it easy to remember, but it produces a consistent batch of gnocchi.

3 pounds russet potatoes (3–4 potatoes)
2 cups flour
1 egg
Pinch salt

1. Rinse the potatoes, place in a large pot, cover with cold water by 3 inches, bring to a boil over medium-high heat, and cook until tender, about 45 minutes. Using a slotted spoon, remove the cooked potatoes to a bowl. While still warm, peel and pass through a food mill set over a large bowl.

2. Make a well in the center of the potatoes. Sprinkle with the flour and salt and crack the egg in the center of the well. Using a fork, pull the potatoes into the egg until mixed in. Fold the mass together to incorporate. Form a ball and knead for 5 minutes.

3. Place a large pot with plenty of water over high heat. Fill a large bowl with ice water and place it near the pot.

4. Break off 6-inch balls of the dough, and, on a cutting board or other surface, roll into a rope ¾ inch in diameter. Cut 1-inch pieces from the rope. When the water boils, dunk the gnocchi in the water and cook until they float, about 1 minute, then remove with a slotted spoon to the ice bath. Repeat until all the dough is used.

5. Drain the gnocchi, toss with oil, and refrigerate until ready to use. You can bag these in small batches and freeze.

Serves 6–8

APPLE RISOTTO

Aside from being scrumptious, a good risotto forces one to get in there and cook. You have to be vigilant and stand in front of the stove over a hot pot of rice, wooden spoon in hand. You and the rice are equal partners, which makes the end result taste that much better. The rice is completed when al dente: just cooked through with a little bit of resistance. It should be pourable and smooth, not thick.

Ingredients:

1 medium acorn squash

1 tablespoon unsalted butter

½ tablespoon sugar

6 cups chicken stock (see sidebar, page 51)

2½ cups apple cider (the extra cider allows for evaporation as it simmers)

¼ cup olive oil

1 small onion, cut into ⅛-inch dice

3 cloves garlic, minced

2 cups Arborio rice

1 cup white wine

½ cup freshly grated Parmesan

3 tablespoons unsalted butter

⅛ teaspoon fresh grated nutmeg

Salt and pepper

Procedure:

1. Preheat oven to 400°F.

2. Halve the squash, scoop out the seeds, and dot the cavity with the butter. Sprinkle with sugar, place on a baking tray, and roast until golden and tender, about 1½ hours. When cool enough to handle, scoop the flesh into a bowl. Reserve.

3. Heat the stock and cider in two small saucepans over low heat. Heat the olive oil in a medium saucepan over medium heat, and then add the onions and garlic. Cook, stirring until translucent, about 4 minutes. Add the rice and stir constantly until it's coated with the fat and has a nutty aroma, 3 minutes.

4. Pour in the wine, stirring continuously. Reduce until dry, then add ½ cup of cider and stir until completely absorbed. Repeat with another ½ cup of cider. From then on, do the same but using only chicken stock, stirring throughout. Taste occasionally to check doneness. When nearly done, add stock in smaller increments.

5. Puree the squash with ¼ cup of the hot cider in a blender or food processor, and fold into the rice. Fold in the cheese and butter, add the nutmeg, season with salt and pepper, and serve in shallow bowls. The rice should be pourable.

Serves 4

{NOTES ON CIDER}

Today's apple cider would, one hundred years ago, be considered apple juice. True apple cider, or hard cider, is a lightly alcoholic beverage made by fermenting apple juice. It was an important, if not central, table beverage of the day. In the agricultural depression of seventeenth-century Britain, many orchardists switched to growing solely cider apples, as they were easier to produce and didn't need to appear uniformly red, round, and unblemished.

The process of true cider making begins with selecting the apples. Cider makers aim for a perfect blend of sugars and acids, and, as with most things apple, it is highly individual: One ciderist's throwaway is another's staple. Generally, cider makers use a blend of varieties, as it is rare to find a single one that contains the perfect mixture of sugars and acids. They also measure the apple's tannins, which give the cider body and richness. Apples high in sugar and tannins are called "bittersweets," while those high in acid and tannins are referred to as "bittertarts."

Whatever the blend, the apples must be ripe. While the tannins and aromas are concentrated primarily in the apple skins, they bloom inside the flesh as the apple ripens. Once the apples are selected, they are ground to a smooth mash, pressed through a fine cheesecloth-like strainer, and then the flavors are blended. The maker tests acid and sugar levels and lets the mix ferment. Its sugars develop into alcohol and carbon dioxide. It is then siphoned and bottled.

You can make a snappy cider at home. Every home brewer has his own method, but the concept is the same: introduce a yeast to preservative-free (mandatory) juice, and seal tightly with any pierced stopper (usually a store-bought airlock, but often a simple balloon with a single pinprick). The hole allows the trapped gases to escape, thereby averting an extremely messy explosion. Ferment unrefrigerated for more than a week, siphon, bottle, refrigerate, and drink. Within the process there is a lot of room to tinker and adjust for personal preference. The longer you ferment, the dryer the product. It will be more like wine. You can use a wild yeast starter, produced by steeping an organic apple peel in apple juice for a few weeks, or you can use a packet of champagne (brewer's) yeast. Because it is an inexact and personal process, we hesitate to provide a recipe and suggest you experiment or search online for ideas.

LAMB AND MASCARPONE RAVIOLI

There are a handful of dishes that Phil has never forgotten. He recalls smells, textures, tastes, surroundings, the time of day, even the weather. One such dish is the *tortellini in brodo* he ate on a family trip to Italy when he was eight. It was a cold day in a tiny hill town with a lone restaurant. He'll never forget that simple dish of toothsome pasta floating in the best-ever chicken stock. Phil had that day in mind when he put together this recipe, which is a bowlful of ravioli and rich lamb stock. Any apple works well: The flavor is meant to be subtle, but use a tart apple for the garnish.

Ingredients:

2 lamb shanks (about 1 pound each)

1 head garlic (halve the garlic widthwise)

3½ cups red wine

4 sprigs rosemary

3½ cups chicken stock (see sidebar, page 51)

⅓ cup peeled and grated apple

1⅓ cups grated Parmesan

¼ cup mascarpone

3 tablespoons ricotta

¼ teaspoon freshly grated nutmeg

1 package wonton skins

1 tablespoon unsalted butter

1 apple

Lemon juice

Pinch ground juniper berries

Procedure:

1. Preheat oven to 325°F.

2. In a large roasting pan, combine the lamb shanks, garlic, wine, rosemary, and stock. Cover tightly with foil and roast until tender, about 2½ hours. Remove and let cool in the liquid.

3. Remove the shanks to a large bowl. Strain the cooking liquid into a separate bowl and refrigerate. Bring a large pot of well-salted water to a boil over high heat.

4. For the filling: Shred the lamb, discard bones, and mix well with the grated apple, ⅓ cup of the Parmesan, mascarpone, ricotta, and nutmeg.

5. Place 1 teaspoon of filling in the center of wonton skin. Fold into a triangle by dabbing the corners with water and touching them together. Place on tray dusted with flour. Repeat.

6. Meanwhile, remove the sauce from the refrigerator, skim the fat, bring to a rolling boil in a small saucepan over medium-high heat, and whisk in the butter.

7. Peel and finely julienne the apple. Toss with the lemon juice and juniper berries.

8. Poach the ravioli until done, about 3 minutes. This should be done in batches. Portion ravioli in shallow bowls and spoon over ⅓ cup of the sauce. Garnish in the center with the apple salad and serve with the reserved cup of grated Parmesan.

Serves 4–6

 SIDES

CAULIFLOWER-APPLE PUREE

Because the acids in apples and other fruits curdle hot milk, you have to add them later in the cooking process. This subtle puree goes well with our aggressively seasoned hangar steak (page 74), but it's even better and more complex the next day.

Ingredients:

1 head cauliflower, trimmed, in 1-inch chunks

4 sprigs thyme

4 cups milk

2 cups peeled, cored, and chopped apples (1-inch chunks)

½ cup heavy cream

1 tablespoon minced chives

Salt and pepper

Procedure:

1. In a medium saucepan over medium-high heat, combine the cauliflower, thyme, and milk. Bring to a simmer, lower heat to medium, add the apples, and simmer 8 to 10 minutes.

2. Using a slotted spoon, transfer the cauliflower and apples (discard the thyme) to a food processor or blender. Add ¼ to ½ cup of the cooking liquid and puree until smooth. (It may look broken, but the cream will bring it back together.) Add the cream, puree, fold in the chives, and season with salt and pepper.

Serves 6

BRAISED RED CABBAGE

Cabbage is underappreciated. Maybe people find it slightly funky, messy to shred, or overly crunchy. Whatever the reason, it's the main player in at least three classic dishes: coleslaw, sauerkraut, and braised red cabbage. These are multiseasonal: think coleslaw at a summer picnic; sauerkraut on a hot dog at a ball game; braised red cabbage with a pork roast on a chilly night. Don't be tempted to remove the cabbage as soon as it wilts. It needs time to develop its full, sturdy flavor.

Ingredients:

3 cups chopped apples, in 1-inch chunks

2 cups apple juice

¼ cup apple cider

½ cup slab bacon, cut to medium dice

½ Spanish onion, cut to medium dice

2 cloves garlic, peeled and sliced thinly

2 tablespoons cider vinegar

1 cup chicken stock (see sidebar, page 51)

1 cup red wine

1 cup cranberry juice

1 sprig rosemary

1 head red cabbage, grated thinly on a mandoline

1½ cups peeled and grated apples

2 tablespoons butter

1 tablespoon grain mustard

¼ cup poppy seeds

Salt and pepper

Procedure:

1. Bring the apple chunks, apple juice, and cider to a boil in a small saucepan over medium-high heat. Cook 15 to 20 minutes or until the liquid has reduced by half. Strain and discard the apples; reserve the liquid.

2. Meanwhile, cook the bacon over medium heat in a large sauté pan until most of its fat is rendered, about 8 minutes. Remove bacon and drain on a paper towel. Keep the fat in the pan.

3. Add the onions and garlic to the bacon fat and sauté over medium heat until browned, 10 to 12 minutes. Add the cider vinegar, scrape the bits off the bottom of the pan with a wooden spoon, and reduce until dry. Pour in the stock, wine, cranberry juice, and reserved apple liquid, then add the rosemary, cabbage, and apples, and simmer for 1½ to 2 hours. Stir in the butter, mustard, and poppy seeds. Season with salt and pepper. Transfer to a platter and top with reserved bacon. Serve.

Serves 4–6

SAGE POLENTA WITH SIMMERED APPLES

A happy accident. One day we were simmering a pot of chopped apples and cider for a sauce. Heading for the trash with a strainerful of cooked apples, we noticed they were wonderfully browned and sweet. We were making polenta at the time and threw them in the pot, where they melted into the hot cornmeal. Our guests ate it up: one more victory for the apple. You need a baking apple, which will soften but retain its shape when reduced in boiling cider.

Ingredients:

2 cups apples, peeled, halved, cored, and cut in 1-inch chunks

2 cups cider

4 cups water

1 cup cornmeal

2 tablespoon mascarpone

⅔ cup Parmesan

Salt and pepper

¼ teaspoon freshly ground nutmeg

1 teaspoon chopped sage

Procedure:

1. Combine apples and cider in a medium saucepan. Bring to a boil over medium-high heat and let reduce until the apples are caramelized and the cider has nearly evaporated, 15 minutes. Remove from heat and cover with foil to keep warm until needed.

2. Meanwhile, in a medium saucepan, bring the water and salt to a boil over medium-high heat. Whisk in the cornmeal in a thin stream, reduce heat to low, and keep whisking until the polenta pulls away from the pot, about 15 minutes. Whisk in the mascarpone, Parmesan, salt, pepper, nutmeg, and sage.

3. Pour polenta into a deep dish, spoon over the apples, and serve.

Serves 6

BROILED LEEKS WITH APPLE VINAIGRETTE

Leeks have a strange organic structure. Although a vegetable, they possess a natural gelatin, which allows them to self-adhere. This property also makes them hearty and able to stand on their own as a side dish, especially when broiled and drizzled with a sauce. They are easier to remove if you tie them in a bundle with butcher's twine before you drop them in the water.

Ingredients:

8 large leeks, white and light green parts only

⅓ cup olive oil

Salt and pepper

1 recipe apple vinaigrette (page 146)

Procedure:

1. Bring a pot of well-salted water to a boil over high heat. Fill a large bowl with ice water. Trim the leek roots and cut each leek in half, stopping at the root so the leek remains intact. Rinse well. Tie the leeks in snug bundles of 4 with kitchen twine (see headnote). Boil leeks until tender, about 6 minutes, and transfer to the ice bath. Once cool, remove and drain, untie the string, and pat dry. Cut in half lengthwise and reserve.

2. Preheat the broiler to high. Oil a baking sheet with 2 tablespoons of olive oil and sprinkle over 2 teaspoons salt. Line the leek halves in a single layer on the baking sheet cut side up and drizzle with remaining olive oil. Season with salt and pepper. Position the baking sheet on a rack 6 inches from the heat source. Broil until lightly charred, about 6 minutes. Serve the leeks on a platter drizzled with the vinaigrette.

Serves 4

These rich, sweet potatoes go well with game, pork, and especially our roast chicken (page 68). Don't smooth the tops as you return the filling to the shells; it should look rustic. As with the butternut squash, use a sweet apple, which complements the natural sugars in the yam.

Ingredients:

¼ cup olive oil

3 large yams (about 1 pound each)

Salt and pepper

1½ cups heavy cream

2 tablespoons unsalted butter

1 tablespoon minced garlic

1½ tablespoons minced thyme

3 cups peeled and diced apples (¼-inch dice)

1 cup bread in 1-inch chunks

1 cup Parmesan in 1-inch chunks

½ cup parsley

Procedure:

1. Preheat oven to 400°F.

2. Line a baking sheet with foil and spread with the olive oil. Roll the yams in the oil to coat, and season well with salt and pepper. Bake until tender, about 1 hour, and remove from oven.

3. Bring the cream to a simmer over medium-high heat in a small saucepan, and whisk in the butter. Reduce heat to medium, add the garlic, thyme, and apples, and season with salt and pepper. Cook until the apples are tender, 8 to 10 minutes.

4. Slice each yam in half and scoop the hot insides into a medium bowl. Fold in the hot cream mixture. Spoon the mixture back into the potato shells.

5. Place the bread, Parmesan, and parsley in a food processor and pulse until fine. Sprinkle the breadcrumb mixture over the potatoes, return to oven, and bake until the yams are lightly browned and crisp, about ½ hour.

Serves 6

SMOKED TROUT MASHED POTATOES

Salty and smoky, smoked trout blends perfectly with a tart apple. Toss the trout with some sour cream and chives, and season with a little black pepper for a great salad. We mixed the trout into soft butter with reduced cider. You could spread the butter on warm bread or whisk it into mashed potatoes as we do here. To use later, roll the butter in plastic and twist the ends to form a sausage shape. Refrigerate until firm and slice. A food mill is mandatory to achieve a smooth potato puree. Serve with the cider-braised short ribs (page 76).

Ingredients:

6 large Yukon Gold potatoes (about 4 pounds)

2 cups cider

1 stick unsalted butter, softened

3½ ounces smoked trout

1 tablespoon Dijon mustard

Salt and pepper

1 cup milk

½ cup heavy cream

Procedure:

1. In a large pot, cover the potatoes with cold water by several inches and bring to a boil. Reduce heat slightly and cook until completely tender but not falling apart, 45 to 50 minutes.

2. Meanwhile, pour the cider into a small pot. Place over high heat and reduce to ¼ cup, 12 minutes. Let cool to room temperature.

3. In a food processor, puree the butter with the trout, mustard, and reduced cider. You'll need to use a rubber spatula to scrape down the sides. Remove the mixture to a medium bowl and mix well. Season lightly with salt and pepper.

4. Drain the potatoes, making sure they are very dry. When just cool enough to handle, peel and pass through a food mill into a large bowl.

5. Return the potatoes to the pot over low heat. Whisk in the milk, cream, and smoked trout butter. Season well with salt and pepper. Serve hot.

Serves: 4–6

DESSERT

BAKLAVA

At once crisp and syrupy, a bite of good baklava is immensely buttery and satisfying. We add a bit of kosher salt to balance the sweetness of the honey and apple. Remember to keep the filo covered with a damp towel, as it dries quickly, but if it flakes, don't worry, just patch it up; the butter acts as a glue. You should use a mandoline fitted with a medium julienne blade, or thinly slice, julienne, and then dice the apple finely.

Ingredients:

6½ ounces pecans

5½ ounces walnuts

¼ cup sugar

¾ pound unsalted butter (3 sticks)

1 apple, peeled

1 tablespoon lemon juice

¼ teaspoon ground nutmeg

¼ teaspoon ground clove

¼ teaspoon ground cinnamon

1 box filo dough, defrosted

Syrup (see sidebar)

Kosher salt

Procedure:

1. Preheat oven to 350°F.

2. Spread nuts in a single layer on a baking sheet, and toast until fragrant, about 6 minutes. Let cool, transfer to a food processor, and pulse several times, until they are coarsely ground. Combine the ground nuts and sugar in a medium bowl, and set aside.

3. Melt the butter in a medium saucepan over low heat.

4. Meanwhile, use a mandoline to cut ⅛-inch slices from the apple. Stack the slices, finely julienne, and dice. Alternatively, use a medium julienne blade and dice. Toss to combine in a small bowl with the lemon juice and spices. Set aside.

5. Using a pastry brush, butter a 17½ x 12½-inch baking sheet. Place one sheet of the filo dough on top of the buttered baking sheet and brush with the butter to cover. Repeat with 5 more sheets of the filo (buttering between each sheet).

6. Butter the top sheet and sprinkle approximately ⅕ of the nut mixture and ⅓ of the apples evenly over the filo. Top with 2 more sheets of filo, buttering in between. Butter the top sheet and sprinkle with another ⅕ of the nuts (no apples). Layer with 2 more sheets of filo, and repeat the process until you have 3 layers of apples and nuts, and 2 layers of only nuts. Finish with a layer of apples and nuts.

7. Top with 4 sheets of filo. Butter the top layer, and cut the baklava into 1-inch squares. Bake for 55 to 65 minutes until golden and crispy. Remove from the oven and cover the hot baklava evenly with the cool syrup (making sure it gets into all the cracks and crevices). Sprinkle lightly with kosher salt. Let cool, uncovered, at room temperature.

8. It will keep, covered, for a week.

Syrup

1 cup sugar

½ cup water

½ cup cider

½ cup honey

Combine all ingredients in a small saucepan over high heat, and bring to a boil. Reduce heat to medium and let simmer for 20 minutes, stirring occasionally. Let cool completely.

APPLE BREAD PUDDING

There's a reason people love bread pudding. What's better than a pan of hot bread and cream, crisp on top, emanating a heady aroma of eggs, cream, and bread? When you dip into this version, you pull out an extra treat—warm apples. We make bread pudding for a lot of events. It's ideal for a sit-down dinner: let the pudding cool, refrigerate until needed, then use a ring mold to cut out individual portions and reheat. Drizzle the honey over each portion rather than the entire pan, as we do when serving family-style. Of course, bread pudding is ideal family-style food. Set it on the table and attack. Any apple will work. If your apples start to fall apart in the simmering water, remove with a slotted spoon (or drain with a colander). They'll melt into the bread and be fine.

Ingredients:

2 tablespoons unsalted butter for greasing the pan

3 cups peeled and diced apples (½-inch dice)

¾ cup water

1 15-ounce loaf challah or brioche, crusts removed, cut into 1-inch dice

2 cups milk

2 cups heavy cream

3 egg yolks

2 eggs

¾ cup sugar

Honey

Procedure:

1. Preheat oven to 350°F.

2. Grease a 12 x 8-inch baking pan with butter. Set aside.

3. In a medium saucepan over medium-high heat, add the apples and water. Bring to a simmer and cook until tender. Drain well and reserve.

4. Spread half the bread evenly on the bottom of the prepared pan, follow with a layer of the apples, and finish with the remaining bread.

5. Add the remaining ingredients except the honey to a medium bowl and whisk vigorously until incorporated. Pour evenly over the bread. Some bread will protrude, which is desired. Press lightly so the top layer of bread soaks up the custard.

6. Bake the pudding until an inserted skewer comes out clean, 45 to 50 minutes. Drizzle all over with honey and serve hot.

Serves 4–6

APPLE CREPES

This recipe is adapted from one of our favorite restaurants, Fleur de Sel, which recently closed. Chef-owner Cyril Renaud, who now owns Bar Breton, serves food that is deceptively uncomplicated. Ever since our first meal at Fleur de Sel, we've raved about this dessert, which is hot, crispy, and buttery. The perfect end to a meal. Adapted from the restaurant by the *New York Times*.

Ingredients:

1⅔ cups flour

4 large eggs

2 cups milk

1½ teaspoons fleur de sel

2 tablespoons sugar

3 tablespoons unsalted butter, melted

FOR THE FILLING AND ASSEMBLY:

4 tablespoons unsalted butter

2 large Granny Smith apples, peeled, cored, and cut into rounds ¼ inch thick

½ cup sugar

Whipped cream, ice cream, or Devonshire cream, for garnish.

Procedure:

1. To prepare batter, place flour in a large mixing bowl. Make a well in the center. Add eggs one at a time, stirring softly in middle to mix egg gradually with flour. Add milk a little at a time until it is smoothly incorporated. Add salt and sugar, and stir to mix. Pass batter through a fine sieve, and then mix in melted butter. Refrigerate up to 12 hours.

2. To assemble, place an 8-inch nonstick omelet or sauté pan over medium heat. Add ½ tablespoon butter and 4 or 5 apple slices. When butter starts to color, turn apple rounds, and pour in ¼ cup crepe batter, tilting pan to coat it evenly.

3. When batter is set and browning at edges, flip crepe with a wide plastic spatula. Top with ½ tablespoon butter. Sprinkle evenly with 1 tablespoon sugar. Brown about 1 minute, and flip again. Immediately transfer to a serving plate. Top with whipped cream, ice cream, or Devonshire cream. Repeat.

Yield: 8 crepes

{A NOTE ON PIE}

"It is a glorious unity . . . by fire fixed in blissful perfection."
—Henry Ward Beecher

Americans aren't the only ones to grasp the perfection of apples baked inside a crust. In his culinary bible, *Le Guide Culinaire,* first published in 1903, Auguste Escoffier offers his *Pommes Chevreuse.* Though a typically elaborate French confection calling for meringue, apricot puree, fancy pastry diamonds, and colored syrup, it's the same concept as American apple pie. In a way, we're fussier than Escofffier about apples baked in a crust. And no group is as fussy as apple growers, who debate less about the crust than they do about the perfect apple with which to fill it.

Some point to charts mandating varieties based on levels of acid, tannin, and sugar. Others elaborate on the art of personal preference gathered from decades of tasting: the tart pie; the sweet pie; the spiced pie; and so on. Some use the classic Rome apple, others a combination of the tart Granny Smith and mild Golden Delicious, all three of which hold their shape in the oven.

In the end, it's fitting that the most reverent words ever written on the apple are this paean to the apple pie: "It is a glorious unity in which sugar gives up its nature as sugar, and butter ceases to be butter, and each flavorsome spice gladly evanesces from its own full nature, that all of them by a common death may rise into the new life of apple pie; not that the apple is no longer apple. It, too, is transformed, and the final pie, though born of apple, sugar, butter, nutmeg, cinnamon, and lemon, is like none of these, but the compound ideal of them all, refined, purified, and by fire fixed in blissful perfection." (Henry Ward Beecher)

APPLESAUCE SPICE CAKE WITH PENUCHE ICING

friend Bridget Johns grew up on a farm and is always introducing us to recipes from her parents and grandparents. Bridget grew up as an original locavore—by necessity rather than fad—and thus the applesauce used in this recipe, of course, should be homemade! And remember that the icing for the spice cake is easier to work with while the icing is still warm.

Ingredients:

FOR THE CAKE:

½ cup unsalted butter, softened

2 cups sugar

2 eggs

2 cups applesauce (page 134)

3 cups cake flour

2 teaspoons baking soda

2 teaspoons cinnamon

½ teaspoon ground allspice

½ teaspoon ground cloves

½ teaspoon nutmeg

1 cup walnuts, finely chopped

FOR THE ICING:

6 tablespoons butter

¾ cup light brown sugar

3 tablespoons half-and-half

1¼ cup confectioners' sugar

Procedure:

1. Preheat oven to 350°F.

2. To make the cake: In a bowl of an electric mixer, fitted with a paddle, cream together butter and sugar. Add eggs and beat until the mixture is light and fluffy. Stir in applesauce to combine.

3. In a separate bowl, sift together flour, baking soda, and spices. Add to applesauce mixture and stir until smooth. Stir in walnuts. Pour batter into a 13 x 9-inch baking pan and bake for 35 to 40 minutes or until a toothpick inserted in the center comes out clean. Remove from oven and let cool.

4. To make the icing: In a small pot, melt butter over medium heat. Stir in brown sugar and bring to a boil. Stirring constantly let boil for 2 minutes. Stir in half-and-half (be careful of sputtering) and bring to a boil. Remove from heat and let cool until lukewarm. Gradually add confectioners' sugar and stir until spreading consistency.

Yield: 1 cake

APPLE CAKE

It may be a cliché that the best recipes are those handed down through generations of family. Think of this cake recipe as a happy cliché. It is adapted from our friends the Mullins and has been in their family for years.

Ingredients:

1⅓ cups vegetable oil

2 cups granulated sugar

2 eggs

3 cups flour

1 teaspoon baking soda

1 teaspoon salt

1 teaspoon cinnamon

¼ teaspoon nutmeg

1 teaspoon vanilla

3 tart apples, peeled, cored, and diced small

Procedure:

1. Preheat oven to 350°F. Grease a 9 x 13-inch baking pan. Line pan with waxed paper and grease the paper.

2. In a large mixing bowl, beat together oil, sugar, and eggs until well blended. Add flour, baking soda, salt, cinnamon, nutmeg, and vanilla. Beat for 2 minutes at medium speed; the dough will be very thick. Remove bowl from mixer and fold in the apples.

3. Pour cake batter into prepared pan, smoothing the top to make an even layer. Bake for 25 minutes, then reduce oven heat to 300°F and continue cooking for 35 to 40 minutes. Cake is done when a toothpick inserted in the center comes out clean.

4. Remove cake from oven and set aside to cool for 5 minutes. Carefully, turn cake out of pan and remove waxed paper. Instantly turn cake back over so that the "pebbly" side of cake is up.

Yield: 1 cake

APPLE PIE

We've served our version of apple pie dozens of times, and it's always a big hit. The cranberry compote adds color as well as a sweet-tart balance. Good baking apples such as Granny Smith and Golden Delicious work very well. In season, we like Idared and Braeburn, but you should experiment. You could also use one apple variety, but because you should use sweet-tart baking apples, which are harder to find, it's more practical (and interesting) to use two or three types. Rest the pie after baking. Otherwise the juices will run. A mandoline helps, as it does whenever you have to cut a bowlful of apples.

Ingredients:

FOR THE CRUST:

2½ cups flour

1 tablespoon sugar

1 teaspoon salt

10 tablespoons cold unsalted butter

7 tablespoons shortening, chilled

6 tablespoons ice water

FOR THE FILLING:

2 cups cranberries

1 cup cranberry juice

1 cup sugar plus 2 tablespoons

4 pounds apples, peeled, cored, quartered, and sliced ⅟₁₆ inch thick on a mandoline

Juice ½ lemon

2 tablespoons flour

½ teaspoon cinnamon plus ¼ teaspoon

4 tablespoons unsalted butter

½ cup milk

Procedure:

TO MAKE THE CRUST:

1. Add the flour, sugar, and salt to a food processor and pulse twice. Dot the butter on top and pulse 5 times for 1 second each. The butter should be the size of small peas. Do the same with the shortening.

2. Turn the dough into a large bowl and, using a spatula or wooden spoon, stir in the water. It is done when you press down and the dough sticks together. Roll into two even discs, wrap each in plastic, and refrigerate for at least 30 minutes.

TO MAKE THE FILLING AND ASSEMBLE:

1. Preheat oven to 400°F. Combine the cranberries, juice, and ½ cup of the sugar in a medium saucepan over medium heat and cook, stirring occasionally, until the liquid is absorbed, 20 minutes. Remove from the heat and let cool.

2. In a large bowl, toss the apple slices with the lemon juice, flour, ½ cup of the sugar, and ½ teaspoon cinnamon. Let sit for 20 minutes.

3. Remove the discs from the refrigerator to soften slightly. On a floured surface roll one of the discs to 1⁄16-inch thickness. Line a 10-inch deep-dish pan with the crust, leaving a slight overhang, and spread the compote over the base. Layer half the apples, top with half the butter, layer the rest, and dot the top with the remaining butter.

4. Roll out the other disc and drape over the top. Pinch together the overhanging crusts and crimp the edges all around. Using a ½-inch ring mold, punch out a circle from the center of the crust.

5. In a small bowl, combine the remaining sugar and cinnamon. Brush the pie with milk and sprinkle with cinnamon sugar. Bake for 50 minutes, or until bubbling. Let the pie sit for at least 30 minutes before slicing.

Yield: 1 double-crust 10-inch pie

FRENCH TOAST TARTE TATIN

Tarte tatin is a delicious blend of crust and supremely caramelized apples. Because they're the centerpiece of tarte tatin, we cook these apples the traditional way. Instead of a pastry crust, we use a thick, eggy slice of brioche French toast. It's a little messy, but delicious. To prevent the sugar from bubbling over, you need a 10-inch pan with 1½-inch sides. A tart apple works to cut the sugar. You must use a good baking apple, which holds its shape during the cooking.

Ingredients:

1 loaf brioche

1 cup milk

4 eggs

1 cup heavy cream

3 tablespoons confectioners' sugar

10 apples, peeled, halved, and cored

¾ cup sugar

4 tablespoons unsalted butter, cut in sixths

½ cup cider syrup, warm (page 147)

Procedure:

1. Preheat oven to 375°F.

2. Cut 4 slices from the brioche loaf, each 1 inch thick. Reserve the remainder for another purpose. In a medium bowl, whisk together the milk and eggs. Place the bread slices in a pan that fits them snugly and soak with the custard. Refrigerate.

3. In a standing mixer or large bowl, whisk the cream and sugar to soft peaks. Refrigerate.

4. Cut a thin slice off one end of the apple halves so that they can stand upright. Sprinkle the sugar evenly over the surface of a large sauté pan and dot the sugar with 2 tablespoons of the butter.

5. Starting on the outside of the sauté pan (see headnote), arrange the apple halves in concentric circles all facing the same direction. Squeeze in as many halves as possible so that they are tightly packed in the pan.

6. Place the pan over medium-high heat. After a few minutes, turn the apples slightly so they don't stick. Eventually, the sugar will melt and caramelize, and the apples will break down

simultaneously. Occasionally, shake the pan gently. You're looking for the sugar to be deeply brown; the apples will be about half the size they were when you started and feel like very soft marshmallows.

7. Remove apples to the oven. Cook 20 minutes. The bottom will be well caramelized, almost burnt.

8. In a large sauté pan over medium-high heat, melt 1 tablespoon of the remaining butter. When hot, add 2 slices of the brioche and cook until browned on both sides, 2 to 3 minutes per side. Remove to a tray, melt the remaining butter, and cook the remaining bread in the same manner.

9. When the apples are done, remove and, using a spatula, thoroughly mix the by now deeply colored apples. It should resemble a smooth puree.

10. To serve, center a brioche slice on each plate, and top with some cooked apples and a dollop of whipped cream. Drizzle a few tablespoons of cider syrup around each plate.

Serves 4

Fried apples are good for breakfast, lunch, and dinner. They're pan-fried and served with French toast or pork chops; batter-dipped, deep-fried apple slices are standard carnival food. Here, we combine the day's bookend meals in one irresistible little fried package. As with most fritters or beignets, it takes a little practice to get the right temperature on your oil. These should be crisp on the outside with a creamy, hearty oatmeal interior. Serve these with bowls of fruit preserves or jams such as our autumn fruit jam (page 149).

Ingredients:

3 cups milk

1½ cups oats

3 cups peeled and grated apples

½ cup black raisins

3 tablespoons brewed espresso

Canola oil for frying

⅓ cup flour

1 teaspoon baking powder

1 cup sugar

Procedure:

1. In a small saucepan over medium heat, bring the milk almost to a boil, being careful not to let it foam over. Whisking constantly, slowly add the oats and cook to oatmeal consistency. Turn into a medium bowl and let cool. Fold in the apples, raisins, and espresso, and refrigerate. Let sit for a few hours or overnight.

2. In a large pot, bring 3 inches of the canola oil to 350°F. Line a baking sheet with paper towels. Remove the oatmeal, bring to room temperature, and fold in the flour and baking powder.

3. Add the sugar to a large bowl. Carefully drop ¼ cup of the batter at a time into the oil and fry until golden on both sides, about 3 to 4 minutes. Cook them in small batches so they get crispy. Remove to the prepared tray to drain then dredge in the sugar bowl. Serve hot.

Yield: 16 pieces

COCONUT PANNA COTTA WITH CARAMEL APPLES

Panna cotta, which means "cooked cream" in Italian, is simple to make, yet looks impressive: a molded dessert, varyingly flavored, with or without a sauce. It should be smooth and light, not firm. Panna cotta can be sweet or savory and paired with any number of items. We often follow the seasons when thinking of accompaniments. Here, we give it the fall/winter treatment and spoon over caramel-coated apples.

Ingredients:

3 tablespoons warm water

2½ teaspoons gelatin

1½ cups whole milk

1½ cups coconut milk

1 teaspoon vanilla extract

¼ cup honey

2 cups cider

2 apples, peeled and turned with a melon baller

2 tablespoons unsalted butter

Zest of 2 limes

Procedure:

1. Pour the water into a small bowl and sprinkle the gelatin on top. Let sit 10 minutes.

2. Meanwhile, pour the milk into a large mixing bowl. Put the coconut milk, vanilla, and honey into a small saucepan and bring to a simmer over medium-high heat. Remove from heat. Whisk the gelatin into the coconut milk until smooth.

3. Pour the mixture into the bowl with the milk and whisk until smooth. Using a ladle, divide the custard into 6 4-ounce ramekins, place on a tray, and refrigerate overnight.

4. Pour the cider into a medium saucepan over medium-high heat and reduce until syrupy, 12 to 15 minutes. Add the apples and butter, reduce the heat to medium, and cook until tender. The cider should coat the apples with a light caramel.

5. Unmold the panna cotta and place one in the center of each plate. Surround with apples and sprinkle the lime zest over top.

Serves 6

GREEN APPLE GELATO

Lauren's junior-year semester in Florence was an eye-opening food adventure down narrow streets and markets hunting down the most delicious paninis, pastas, and ribbolita (a hearty bread-based vegetable soup). She also discovered green apple gelato. Each bite is like savoring a perfectly ripe apple just off the tree. There are shreds of apple, which provide a wonderful texture and authenticity. Traditionally, fruit gelatos are dairy-free, resembling sorbet rather than ice cream. Vitamin C keeps the juice green.

Ingredients:

½ cup sugar

1¼ cups water

4 Granny Smith apples

1 teaspoon vitamin C powder

Procedure:

1. Combine the sugar and water in a small saucepan and bring to a boil over medium-high heat. Stir occasionally, boiling the mixture until the sugar is completely dissolved.

2. Meanwhile, pass 3 of the apples through a juicer into a small container. Skim foam and stir in the vitamin C powder.

3. Core and chop the remaining apple. In a food processor, pulse to a chunky puree, 5 to 6 pulses.

4. Combine the hot sugar mixture, apple juice, and pureed apples in a container. Refrigerate overnight, or until completely chilled.

5. Transfer the apple mixture to an ice cream maker and process according to the manufacturer's instructions. Transfer to a plastic container and freeze.

Yield: 1 quart

APPLE ICE CREAM

This basic ice cream is mixed with lightly cooked apple cubes. Unlike, say, bits of chocolate or nuts, the apples transform in the freezer and become slightly icy, adding a surprising texture. Add them near the end of the freezing process.

Ingredients:

1 cup milk

1½ cups heavy cream

½ cup sugar

3 egg yolks

1 tablespoon butter

2 tablespoons sugar

2 apples, cut into ½-inch dice

Procedure:

1. Fill a large bowl with ice water.

2. Bring milk, cream, and ¼ cup of the sugar to near boil in a medium saucepan over medium-high heat. Meanwhile, whisk the yolks in a large bowl with the remaining ¼ cup sugar until pale in color.

3. Slowly drizzle a ladleful of the hot mixture into the yolks, whisking vigorously. Repeat 2 more times, then slowly pour the egg mixture back into the pot, again whisking vigorously. Whisk on medium heat until the mixture thickens slightly, 4 to 5 minutes.

4. Strain the ice cream base into a bowl set in the ice bath, cool, then pour into a plastic container. Cover and refrigerate overnight.

5. Melt the butter in a medium sauté pan over medium heat and sprinkle over the sugar. Add the apples and cook until tender, about 3 minutes. Remove to a bowl, and refrigerate.

6. The next day, pour the mixture into the ice cream machine and process according to the manufacturer's directions until nearly done, then add the apples through the feed tube and continue processing until done. Turn into a container and place in freezer.

Yield: 3 cups

APPLE JACKS ICE CREAM

It may take a superhuman palate to detect the apple juice in Apple Jacks, but it's in there. However, it doesn't take a superhuman palate to pick up the memorable flavor of cereal-soaked milk. We thought of this while watching our son lap up the last remnants of milk at the bottom of his cereal bowl.

Ingredients:

1½ cups milk

1½ cups heavy cream

3 cups Apple Jacks

4 egg yolks

½ cup sugar

Procedure:

1. Fill a large bowl with ice water.

2. Combine the milk, cream, and 2 cups Apple Jacks in a bowl. Let stand for 1 hour, or cover and refrigerate overnight.

3. Strain the infused mixture into a medium pot. Bring to a simmer over medium heat.

4. Meanwhile, in a medium-size bowl, whisk the yolks and sugar until pale and creamy.

5. Whisking vigorously, slowly drizzle one ladleful of the milk mixture into the eggs. Repeat 2 more times. Slowly pour the mixture back into the remaining milk and continually whisk over low heat until mixture has thickened, 4 to 5 minutes. Strain through a fine mesh strainer into a bowl and set inside the ice bath to cool. Cover and refrigerate overnight.

6. Turn the base into an ice cream maker and follow the manufacturer's instructions. Serve topped with remaining Apple Jacks.

Yield: 3 cups

Apples and cheese are a classic combination: The crisp juice cuts through the rich dairy. Because the best cheese plates let the cheeses speak for themselves, you should keep it simple. Find the best you can find, serve with sliced apples, maybe some nuts, and plain crackers.

There are no firm rules. These are just suggestions. Pick three to six cheeses and lay them out in a progression from mild to strong. If your first taste is a powerful blue cheese, it will ruin your palate for the remaining offerings. Usually you end with a firm cheese, but you can finish with a soft cheese, so long as it is pronounced in flavor. For an individual plate, the portions should be small, maybe two bites of each cheese. If you can, search out a local cheese monger who sells a wider variety than the supermarket, although you can find perfectly acceptable cheeses there as well.

People have wildly varying palates: One person's stinky cheese is another's pleasantly aromatic. Keep tasting. It's a delicious journey.

Some ideas:

- Brin d'Amour, Manchego, Montgomery Cheddar, Roquefort
- Selles sur Cher, Tete de Moine, Appenzeller, Parmigiana Reggiano
- Boucheron, Gruyère, St. Marcellin, Taleggio
- Robiola tre Latti, Ardrahan, Roncal, Queso la Serena

SAUCES AND CONDIMENTS

Applesauce seems so simple, yet it illustrates a tenet of cooking with apples. Because the apple's distinct taste is contained near the peel and in the juice, a cooked apple is relatively bland and less "appley." A pinch of sugar reintroduces the original flavor; when sautéing apples in butter—even a tart apple—we sprinkle up to a tablespoon of sugar over the butter before adding the apples to the pan. However, because the pot juices are reintroduced when making applesauce, the sugar is optional, so feel free to sweeten to taste. We like a sweet apple.

Ingredients:

8 cups apples, peeled, cored, and chopped

Juice of 1 lemon

1½ cups water

3 tablespoons sugar

Procedure:

Add all the ingredients to a medium pot over medium heat. Simmer for 20 minutes or until tender. Puree in a blender or food processor.

Yield: 4 cups

BROWN BUTTER APPLESAUCE

With one culinary twirl, you can reinvent an ancient food from baby food or side dish to nutty, sophisticated condiment.

Ingredients:

1 recipe applesauce (previous page)

4 tablespoons unsalted butter

Procedure:

Pour applesauce into a blender or food processor. Melt the butter in a small sauté pan over medium-high heat. Cook until the butter is browned and nutty, 3 to 4 minutes. Pour into the blender with the applesauce and puree.

Yield: 4 cups

APPLE BUTTER

Apples have a lot of natural pectin, which gives apple butter its characteristic spreadable density. It's also one of our oldest foods; the settlers made it an all-day and -night event, chopping barrels of apples and simmering overnight. Many eighteenth-century cooks had a similar approach: boiling and reducing cider then adding the apples. Use a good, sweet baking apple.

Ingredients:

4 pounds apples, unpeeled, cut in chunks

6 cups cider

Procedure:

1. Combine the apples and cider in a large, heavy pot over medium-high heat. Simmer until soft.

2. Run the apples through a food mill into a large bowl. Return applesauce to pot and simmer over a low flame. Stir occasionally to prevent scorching. Cook until the mixture is thickened, 4 to 5 hours.

Yield: 4 cups

APPLE-PEAR PUREE

There's a reason why poached pears are far more common than poached apples. Pears are dryer and tend to hold together in simmering liquid. While you can, of course, poach apples, you need to keep an eye on them, as they tend to become mushy. Because we're aiming for a denser puree, for this dish it's more practical to bake them in the oven with the pears. In any event, you want to use a baking apple such as a Jonathan. We fold the puree into mac 'n cheese (page 94).

Ingredients:

1 cup sugar

Juice 1 lemon

2 baking apples, peeled, halved, and cored

2 pears, peeled, halved, and cored

Procedure:

1. Preheat oven to 350°F.

2. Spread the sugar over the bottom of a 10-inch round baking pan and pour the lemon juice over the sugar. Top with the fruit, cut-side down. They should fit snugly. Bake until tender, about 1 hour.

3. Place the fruit into a food processor and puree.

Yield: 2 cups

APPLE CHUTNEY

We make our own chutneys, often using Indian flavors (see our quesadillas), as store-bought chutneys tend to be cloying and syrupy. Chutneys are versatile. They don't have to be Indian, and they accompany a lot of foods. Ours is jamlike with some visible chunks for texture. A sweet apple is appropriate.

Ingredients:

2 tablespoons unsalted butter

¼ teaspoon ground cumin

¼ teaspoon ground coriander

¼ teaspoon cayenne pepper

3 pounds apples, peeled, cored, and cut in ½-inch dice (about 6 apples)

1 cup chopped dried apricots

1 cup raisins

1 cup grated carrot

½ tablespoon brown sugar

2 teaspoons salt

Juice ½ lemon

½ cup water

½ cup orange juice

¼ cup apple cider

Procedure:

1. Melt the butter in a medium saucepan over medium heat. Add the spices and fry 30 seconds. Introduce the remaining ingredients.

2. Mix well and reduce heat to medium-low. Stir frequently. The apples will break down and the flavors will meld, 45 minutes to 1 hour. The chutney should be spreadable and almost jamlike.

Yield: 4 cups

Anyone familiar with the Passover seder will recognize charoset. It's the side dish meant to represent the mortar used by the Jews to build their homes while under exile in Egypt. You eat it with matzo during the premeal prayers, sometimes with a little horseradish. Our friend Matt Salganick swears by his father's charoset, which we adapted. You can omit the raisins if you have raisin issues.

Ingredients:

1 apple (¼-inch dice)

½ cup golden raisins

6 tablespoons sweet kosher wine, such as Manischewitz

½ cup walnuts, coarsely chopped

¼ teaspoon freshly grated nutmeg or ground cinnamon

Procedure:

Mix the fruit and wine in a small bowl to macerate for 1 hour. Add the nuts and nutmeg. Can be served immediately or made one day ahead.

Yield: 2 cups

APPLE TZATZIKI

Sauce or side? Tzatziki is a Greek dip usually served with pita triangles. Many cultures have their own version of yogurt dip (Indians use mustard seeds for garlic). We make them at home all the time; they're simple to put together, yet interesting and completely addictive. As with our *giardiniera,* the apple will convert purists. Use a tart apple.

Ingredients:

1 apple, peeled

2 Kirby cucumbers or 1 medium cucumber, peeled and seeded

Juice of 1 lemon

⅓ cup chopped fresh dill

1 garlic clove, minced

2 cups Greek yogurt

1 teaspoon salt

Procedure:

1. Grate the apple and cucumbers on a cheese grater. Squeeze out as much liquid as possible with your hands. Place in a medium bowl.

2. Add lemon juice, dill, garlic, yogurt, and salt and stir until combined. Cover and refrigerate until needed.

Yield: 2½ cups

APPLE *GIARDINIERA*

Giardiniera is technically a mix of vegetables marinated in a vinegar-based brine. In Chicago, *giardiniera* is almost a religion. The vegetables are chopped small, marinated primarily in oil, and served on beef sandwiches. Chicagoans might scoff at adding apples, but they lend a balance to the sharp condiment. A sweet-tart apple works well.

Ingredients:

1 rib celery, sliced thinly

1 medium carrot, peeled and sliced thinly

1 apple, small dice

1 jalapeño, sliced in thin rounds

1 small onion, cut into small dice

1 clove garlic, minced

1 teaspoon red pepper flakes

1 teaspoon dried oregano

2 tablespoons chopped kalamata olives

¼ cup cider vinegar

1 cup olive oil

Salt

Procedure:

Mix all the ingredients in a large bowl. Season well with salt and refrigerate. Will last several days.

Yield: 2 cups

SWEET-AND-SOUR APPLES

Out of season, it's hard to find a spectacularly spicy apple with a heady sweet-tart balance. However, dunking julienned apples in a sweet-sour brine mimics the flesh of a good sweet-tart apple, donating some acid to a sweet apple and some sweet to a tart apple. We serve these a lot with heavier items such as bacon, duck, and chicken liver. They keep three to four days.

Ingredients:

1 cup sugar

1 cup cider vinegar

1 tablespoon coriander seed

1 teaspoon crushed red pepper

1 bay leaf

2 cups peeled, julienned apples
(⅛-inch julienne)

Procedure:

1. Place all the ingredients except the apples in a small saucepan over medium heat, stirring occasionally until the sugar dissolves. Remove from heat and let cool.

2. Pour sugar and vinegar mixture over apples. Refrigerate, covered.

Yield: 2 cups

APPLE KIMCHEE

A recipe from our friend Bob Kim, whose aunt prepares this simple dish. Kimchee is an extremely spicy and delicious fermented condiment, usually made from cabbage, which is ubiquitous in Korea. Part of the kimchee mystique is the practice of burying it underground in clay containers to let it ferment. But there are many kimchees meant to be eaten right away. Serve it in small bowls to mix with rice, or as a condiment with grilled meats. This will last for two days covered and refrigerated.

Ingredients:

2 scallions, trimmed

2 cups peeled, diced apples (½-inch dice)

2 tablespoons fish sauce

2 teaspoons crushed red pepper

2 cloves garlic, peeled and crushed

2 teaspoons toasted sesame seeds

Procedure:

1. Cut the scallions, white part only, into ½-inch-long pieces.

2. Mix all ingredients thoroughly in a bowl or plastic container, cover, and refrigerate for 3 hours.

Yield: 2 cups

CIDER AIOLI

The distinctive sugar of reduced cider will make you think twice about mixing your morning yogurt with honey. We drizzle this on pancakes or blueberries and keep it in the fridge, ready to swoop in for an occasional fingerful. For events we spoon it over fresh fruit and serve it in bowls as a dip for fried chicken (page 66).

Ingredients:

2 cups cider

1½ cups sour cream or crème fraîche

Procedure:

1. In a medium saucepan over high heat, bring cider to a boil and reduce until syrupy, about 12 minutes. You should have ¼ cup. Let cool.

2. Whisk cider reduction with sour cream or crème fraîche.

Yield: 2 cups

APPLE-CHIVE DIPPING SAUCE

Pam Real Thai is a tiny restaurant on Ninth Avenue run by Pam, a sprightly woman who also does the cooking in an equally tiny kitchen. She serves crisp duck, steamed mussels, barbecued pork, and a superb crisp chive dumpling, its exterior holding a bright green, oniony parcel of sautéed garlic chives. We put together a simple sauce inspired by that dumpling. It's a balance of chives, ginger, apple, and oil, and is great spooned over steamed shellfish. Any crisp apple works well.

Ingredients:

¼ cup peeled, diced apple (⅛-inch dice)

1½ teaspoons peeled, minced ginger

1½ tablespoons minced chives

1 tablespoon rice vinegar

½ cup canola oil

Pinch salt

Procedure:

Combine all ingredients in a small bowl and stir. Serve immediately.

Yield: ½ cup

APPLE VINAIGRETTE

One of the easiest vinaigrettes to make: throw everything in a blender and don't worry about the sauce breaking, as the apple acts as an emulsifier. A sweet or sweet-tart apple works.

Ingredients:

1 teaspoon chopped garlic

½ teaspoon chopped shallot

1 cup chopped apple, peeled

2 tablespoons balsamic vinegar

⅔ cup olive oil

Salt and pepper

Procedure:

Combine all ingredients except salt and pepper in a blender and pulse until smooth. Season.

Yield: ¾ cup

Apple-Pomegranate Vinaigrette

A few tablespoons of reduced pomegranate juice turns the apple vinaigrette a mellow pinkish-red and adds a sour-sweetness to the sugar in the apple.

1 cup pomegranate juice

1. Bring juice to a boil in a small saucepan over high heat. Reduce to syrupy, 9 to 10 minutes.

2. Add 2 tablespoons of the syrup to the blender containing the vinaigrette and pulse until smooth. Season with salt and pepper.

CIDER SYRUP

Reduced apple cider has a more complex sweetness than honey or (we think) any other reduced juice. If you only need a little bit, such as when making a sauce or vinaigrette, you need simply boil down a pot of cider. If you're looking to douse your pancakes, cook it with sugar, which acts as a thickener and increases the yield.

Ingredients:

2 tablespoons unsalted butter

3 cups cider

1 cup sugar

Procedure:

In a medium pot over medium heat, melt the butter. Add the cider and sugar, and boil until sugar is dissolved and the mixture has thickened, 12 to 15 minutes. Will keep in the refrigerator for several months.

Yield: 1½ cups

CIDER VINEGAR BARBECUE SAUCE

During a three-week road trip through the South, we ate a lot of great barbecue, but we'll always remember the ribs and chicken we found in Duck, North Carolina, where the smoky, fall-off-the-bone ribs are accompanied by squeeze bottles of that spicy, vinegary sauce characteristic of Carolina 'Q.

Ingredients:

½ cup honey

1 cup apple juice

1 cup cider vinegar

2 tablespoons brown sugar

½ cup ketchup

1 teaspoon red pepper flakes

Procedure:

1. In a medium pot over medium-high heat, cook the honey until deeply amber, 4 to 5 minutes.

2. Pour in the apple juice (be careful, it will sputter) and reduce by half. Reduce heat to medium and whisk in the vinegar, sugar, ketchup, and red pepper flakes.

3. Simmer for 15 minutes, remove from heat, and let cool.

Yield: 2 cups

AUTUMN FRUIT JAM

While on the Cape, we visited the Thornton Burgess Society, a small environmental education center in Sandwich, Massachusetts. Its garden trails bloom with wildflowers, and its Jam Kitchen produces some of the finest Jams and Jellies we've ever tasted. The autumn fruit jam comes directly from the Jam Kitchen's cookbook, which also gives extensive canning directions (page 14).

Ingredients:

½ pound apples, peeled, halved, cored, and cut in ½-inch chunks

½ pound plums, peeled, halved, cored, and cut in ½-inch chunks

½ pound pears, washed, pitted, and cut in ½-inch chunks

½ cup water

4 cups sugar

Procedure:

1. In a medium pot over medium heat, cook the fruit and water until softened, about 20 minutes.

2. Add sugar and stir until dissolved. Increase heat and boil rapidly until thick and glossy. Let settle, then stir to distribute fruit.

3. Skim foam from the top. Store in a plastic container and refrigerate, or in sterilized jars and store up to a year on the shelf.

Yield: 1–1½ quarts

COCKTAILS

BONDED IN SPICE

Apples present a challenge to drink makers. They can't be squeezed like a grapefruit, pureed like a peach, or crushed like a raspberry, which is why bartenders rely on their liquid by-products such as apple juice, apple cider, and calvados. It takes skill to balance these ingredients. Usually a drink is too boozy or dominated by heavy Christmas spice. One day, we were at the bar in the Crosby Hotel, a London boutique hotel that opened recently in SoHo. Its apple cocktail was unbelievable: heady with calvados but lightened by apple juice and brightened by a lot of cayenne and hot sauce. Gerry Corcoran, its creator, was kind enough to donate the recipe.

Ingredients:

2 ounces Laird's bonded apple brandy

½ ounce honey syrup (1 to 1 ratio honey to water)

¼ ounce St. Elizabeth Allspice

¾ ounce fresh lime juice

4 dashes Cholula hot sauce

1 Granny Smith apple, halved and cored

Cayenne pepper

Procedure:

1. Combine the first 5 ingredients in a cocktail shaker with ice. Shake and strain over fresh ice in a highball glass.

2. Slice the apple halves lengthwise into ⅛-inch-thick slices. Fan 3 slices over the top of the glass, securing with a toothpick. Dust with cayenne pepper. Serve.

Yield: 1 drink

SPARKLING APPLES

Our bartender, Laurelle Rethke, pours a mean cocktail. She thought up these next two, one refreshing, one hot, both sleek and urbane. Prosecco is a dry, sparkling white wine. It's a less expensive—but perfectly fine—substitute for champagne.

Ingredients:

3 cups unpeeled, cored, chopped apples

2 cups apple juice

1 tablespoon sugar

Champagne or Prosecco

1 Granny Smith apple, unpeeled, cut into ¼-inch dice

Ground cinnamon

Procedure:

1. In a small saucepan over medium-high heat, bring apples, juice, and sugar to a boil. Lower the heat to medium and simmer until reduced by half, 15 to 20 minutes. Strain and refrigerate until cold.

2. Pour 4 ounces Champagne or Prosecco into a cold champagne flute, and top with 2 ounces of the strained juice. Drop in 1 tablespoon of the diced Granny Smith apple and sprinkle with a pinch of cinnamon.

Yield: 4 drinks

Southern Comfort is pre-spiced, but when you add hot cider and a touch of cinnamon and cloves, it becomes a true cold weather drink. In a highball glass, the Comfort with Apples warms your hands and belly.

Ingredients:

2 cups cider

4 cloves

1 cinnamon stick

Southern Comfort

Procedure:

1. In a small saucepan bring the cider, cloves, and cinnamon stick to a boil. Remove from heat.

2. In highball glasses or mugs, combine 3 parts cider to 1 part Southern Comfort. Serve hot.

Yield: 4 drinks

SOURCES

Annie Proulx and Lew Nichols. *Making, Using and Enjoying Sweet & Hard Cider.* North Adams, Massachusetts: Storey Publishing, 1983.

Beth Hanson, ed. *The Best Apples to Buy and Grow.* Brooklyn, New York: Brooklyn Botanic Garden, 2005.

Doctor John A. Warder. *American Pomology.* New York: Orange Judd & Company, 1867.

Dr. James Thacher. *The American Orchardist: Or, a Practical Treatise on the Culture and Management of Apple and Other Fruit Trees,* 2d. edition. Boston: Joseph W. Ingraham, 1822.

Frank Browning. *Apples.* New York: North Point Press, 1998.

H. L. Cracknell and R. J. Kaufmann. *Escoffier, The Complete Guide to the Art of Modern Cookery.* Wiley, 1979.

Henry D. Thoreau. *Wild Apples and Other Natural History Essays,* William Rossi, ed. Athens, Georgia: University of Georgia Press, 2002.

Joan Morgan and Alison Richards. *The New Book of Apples.* London: Ebury Press, 1993.

Lex Hesler. *The Manual of Fruit Diseases.* The Macmillan Company, 1917.

Roger Yepsen. *Apples.* New York: W. W. Norton, 1994.

S. A. Beach. *The Apples of New York*, vols. 1 and 2. Albany, New York: J. B. Lyon Co., 1905.

Sereno Edwards Todd. *The Apple Culturist: A Complete Treatise for the Practical Pomologist.* New York: Harper & Bros., 1871.

The Encyclopedia of Practical Horticulture vol. 4, Granville Lowther, editor-in-chief. Yakima, Washington: Encyclopedia of Horticulture Corporation, 1914.

Thornton Burgess Society. *Green Briar Jam Kitchen Cook Book,* 2003.

W. C. Flagg. The Apple, *Missouri Yearbook of Agriculture: 1867 Annual Report,* 1867.

Waverly Root. *The Food of France.* Vintage Books, 1958.

William Shakespeare. *A Winter's Tale,* IV. 89.

INDEX

ABOUT THE AUTHORS

Prior to opening their Manhattan catering company, 2 Peas & A Pot, Phil and Lauren Rubin worked in several restaurants, including Tribeca Grill, Cafe Luxembourg, and Union Pacific. Lauren has also worked as a personal chef and recipe tester at *Good Housekeeping*. They are graduates of the Institute of Culinary Education in New York City, where they live with their son, Henry.